# Bulletin Boards
# To Brag About

For Tom
and his dedication to
books and their authors

ISBN 0-673-18280-0

1  2  3  4  5  6-MAL-90  89  88  87  86  85

# Contents

# Acknowledgements

ulletin Boards to Brag About was made possible by many individuals. Ideas on the pages that follow are based on actual bulletin board displays created by teacher-education students enrolled in my media classes over the years. To name them all is not possible, but to praise them for their creativity and skill is. The book was developed because Tom Sherman insisted that these ideas were too good not to share. Others played the roles of teacher, critic, and interpreter.

Special thanks goes to Jeanetta Graham whose ideas, endless patience, and red pen helped to shape the manuscript. Only a true friend would volunteer to remain involved from as far away as New Zealand.

My gratitude goes to Euola Cox for carefully checking the manuscript to ensure that the ideas were nonsexist and appropriately represented the diversity of cultures in our nation.

Roxy Saavedra patiently tutored me and my microcomputer as we labored to become acquainted with a professional word-processing program. What did writers do before the microprocessor?

Preliminary art work was contributed by Dede Gatewood, who converted slides to line drawings; Ruth Yos added to this collection of original drawings; and Nico Cameron, although not trained as an artist, gave it her all to complete the last few sketches. The ideas she brought with her from working in the schools helped add just the right finishing touches.

This book belongs to all of us and to the many supportive colleagues and friends who offered occasional suggestions and constant encouragement.

# Using This Book

Teachers of grades K–6 are constantly looking for ways to motivate students and to make the classroom more attractive. Bulletin boards, especially those using a fresh approach, spark student interest and extend an exciting invitation to learn. It is with this in mind that this book was written. The ideas presented here differ from those found in other sources because they describe displays that are meant to attract attention and arouse learner enthusiasm through the liberal use of three-dimensional objects. Incorporating all types of real items, an assortment of containers, and clothing of a variety of textures is encouraged. Since dimensionality in classroom displays is seldom found, the ideas in this book are special; yet they are far from complex. Because they lack a great deal of detail, they can be reproduced easily with the aid of an opaque or overhead projector. Where applicable, tips are offered for saving money on the materials used.

Every attempt has been made to include all the information needed to reproduce each board illustrated. Suggestions are offered for colors and materials to use, as well as hints on how to construct each display. Where appropriate, ideas for getting students involved in making or using the display are also presented.

At first glance, it may appear that there are only fifty bulletin board ideas in this book. Upon careful inspection, however, it becomes evident that there are actually close to two hundred. After the description of each board is given, suggestions are offered for making simple adaptations, thereby extending the basic display for use in other subject areas and different grade levels. What you see in this book should give you many ideas for adaptations of your own.

## Motivation

The impact of the electronic age on today's school-age children cannot be overemphasized. Nor can it be ignored. The average child now spends approximately six-and-a-half hours a day in the company of a television set that delivers a steady stream of loud music, fast-moving pictures, winning animals who dance and sing to catchy jingles, and super heroes who move to the rhythm of bangs, pows, and zings. These are children who have grown up with high-tech video games that munch, crunch, and splat. A trip to the supermarket offers the likes of Cap'n Crunch, Mr. Clean, Tony the Tiger, and many other pop-culture images. Children sleep on sheets that are decorated with brightly colored cartoon characters and popular culture figures; these same images appear again on their lunch boxes, T-shirts, notebooks, snuggle sacks, bath towels, and even their underwear. Yes, the children of today live in a highly stimulating world.

It seems only logical that teachers should attempt to create a stimulating classroom environment that capitalizes on some of the out-of-school influences that fascinate children. One way to accomplish this is through the use of attractive instructional displays. A bulletin board should be an interest arouser, an attention getter, in short, a motivator. True, bulletin board displays may serve nothing more than a decorative function, making the classroom an inviting place, but as a rule, they should do much more. First, they should say, "Hey, there are neat things going on in this classroom." By making instruction seem attractive and interesting, children will feel that they are being invited to participate in something exciting and important. A simple, attractive, colorful, and "with it" display can do just that.

Above all, bulletin boards should instruct. They can be used to introduce a new concept or unit of instruction; or they can serve as a vehicle for delivering information. One of the most productive types of instructional displays is the manipulative board, where children work individually or in small groups to master a particular skill. Imagine a board displaying three fluffy chicks sitting on a nest of straw. In one corner of the display hangs a set of paper worms on which math problems are written. Children try to solve the problems and then check to see if their answers are correct by turning the worms over. If their answers are correct, the children get to "feed" the chicks by hanging their worms on the board. This is an engaging way to help students move toward mastery of the basics. Displays can also be used to summarize the material covered in a unit of instruction or a related set of lessons; or they can serve as a vehicle for displaying the results of instruction by giving children a chance to show others what they have learned.

In addition to providing opportunities for cognitive growth, the elementary school curriculum must focus on affective learning experiences, especially those involving acceptable behaviors in groups and positive interpersonal skills. Here, too, classroom displays are helpful.

Your main objective is to create bulletin board displays that work for you, that help you do a better job of teaching and organizing the classroom. To achieve the latter, you may want to post the day's or week's schedule in an attractive display. This will provide a framework within which the students can work, allowing them to make decisions about how to manage their time and helping them to be at a designated location at a specified time. Conveying to students that they are responsible individuals who are capable of taking care of themselves is important.

We have all seen bulletin boards haphazardly strewn with any number of student papers. Trying to make sense of such displays often causes so much confusion that it just does not seem worth the effort. However, a board that is specially designed for the purpose of displaying student work motivates children to do their best. For example, suppose that the children in your class were assigned to use their language arts skills to write a short story about their favorite food. Instead of making this just another "assignment," consider how much more exciting and meaningful it would be to the students to write their stories on circles of lined paper and then display them on top of cookie-shaped cutouts that are then placed in the arms of a shaggy, colorful Cookie Monster large enough to cover an entire bulletin board. Add the caption "I Love Cookies," and what child could resist doing the best job possible?

## Multicultural and Nonsexist Content

We live in a multiethnic society where minorities and females now pursue occupations that previously were open only to white males. Today, growing numbers of women and members of various ethnic groups are making important contributions in every area—business, politics, literature, science, industry, and so forth. Little girls participate actively in all sorts of sports; little boys mix up batches of chocolate chip cookies.

Throughout our history, individuals from all cultures have been inventors, educators, physicians, and public servants. Yet traditionally, it has been the Anglo male who has received most of the attention in our classrooms. How many children have learned about the contributions of such Americans as Mathew Henson, Mary McLeod Bethune, and Ramona Banuelos? How many have been taught that Will Rogers was a Cherokee Indian, that Joan Baez is Hispanic?

When choosing instructional materials, teachers must be careful to reject those that are stereotypic and that do not accurately represent the true character of American society. Unfortunately, some manufacturers of commercial bulletin board display materials have failed to recognize the need for more egalitarian educational tools and have continued to produce "cutesy" items showing Anglo characters in "traditional" roles. Teachers who create their own displays can avoid these kinds of mistakes.

Males and females from every ethnic background can be shown participating in all types of activities, and objects from Hispanic, African, Oriental, and many other cultures can be prominently displayed.

There are two major reasons for giving classroom learning materials this multicultural focus. First, in many American classrooms, the majority of the students belong to one particular ethnic group. These children share a common experiential background that is unique to their culture. This is reflected in the foods they eat, in the stories they hear, in their attitudes toward their family, in the way they celebrate festive occasions, and even in their mode of dress. This is what they know and relate to best. Yet when these children go to school, what they see and hear may seem very alien to them—and to the life they know at home. To facilitate learning, theorists have supported the notion of starting with the familiar and then moving toward the less familiar. This can be accomplished by using familiar objects to help teach a specific set of concepts, skills, attitudes, and appreciations. For example, if the instructional goal is for children to develop skills in solving story problems, for the Hispanic child it will be much more meaningful to have a problem that deals with *pan dulce* (sweet bread) than with hot cross buns or with *pinatas* instead of with grab bags.

The second reason for including multicultural content in all areas of instruction is twofold. It says to children of a particular heritage that their people have contributed in meaningful ways to this country. This gives children a feeling of pride and something to emulate. Furthermore, by focusing on the contributions of people of all cultures and on what makes each group unique, we let children know that people of all ethnic backgrounds are important and that our cultural differences are what account for our country's colorful diversity and richness.

Using nonsexist, culturally representative instructional materials is not difficult and can become second nature for all teachers. Some suggestions about how to accomplish this are found in the bulletin board ideas on the following pages. People's faces are white, brown, and black; foods include tacos, bagels, spaghetti, rice, beans; books displayed are written by and about individuals of diverse backgrounds. We hope some day it will not be necessary to remind teachers of the need to make a conscientious effort to provide multiethnic and nonsexist instruction.

## The Effective Display

One has only to look in department store windows or at magazine ads to see what an effective visual display looks like. People who design these visual messages spend many years learning their craft. Even though most teachers do not have similar training, they can learn to create well-designed bulletin board displays by following a few basic guidelines. You will find these useful when you attempt to adapt the displays in this book to your specific needs or when you decide to design your own displays from scratch. Remembering and using the following guidelines will result in display that have that "expert" or "professional" look.

Since bulletin boards are visual display devices, the material contained in them should be mainly visual; words should be used to complement the message and help support the visual. One common mistake made by the amateur bulletin board designer is to allow the size or number of words to overpower the visual elements in the display—a serious misuse of the medium.

If you leaf through the pages of this book, you will probably say to yourself, "These boards don't look very hard to make; why didn't I think of that?" That's just the point. First of all, a basic visual display—in this case, a bulletin board display—is simple. It contains one idea, its purpose being to communicate one major point, no more. Additionally, a good display is uncluttered. Guard against using a lot of small objects in displays. Only the experts can arrange all those things in a way that looks pleasing. Simplicity in the use of color is also important in creating an effective display. Too many colors will confuse the message rather than add to it.

An effective display is unified. Everything in it contributes to the message being communicated. Therefore, all colors, shapes, textures, and objects belong and function together. Unity is achieved by establishing an attractive color scheme and avoiding the use of conflicting shapes or textures. Repeating one color when bordering pictures or verbal information will help to achieve this unity. Even surrounding the entire display with a border helps give the impression of wholeness. Borders may be made simply from strips of bulletin board paper. Crepe paper strips may be used too, but may droop if the humidity rises. Scalloped or serrated borders require the repetition of a pattern. A series of footballs, leaves, or stars cut in paper-doll fashion create more complex edgings.

A good display has emphasis. One large dominant object in the display will achieve this, as is demonstrated in most of the bulletin boards illustrated in this book. An unusual shape or color will accomplish this, too.

A good display is balanced. The board's surface is utilized so that one side or one part does not appear to have most of the display elements on it. There are two types of balance: formal, or symmetrical, and informal. In the formal layout, the objects on the board are arranged so that one half of the display is a mirror image, or exact duplicate of the other half. Elements on the board are laid out in a repetitive fashion (for example, three horizontal rows of four pictures of equal size). Formal balance should be avoided because it is static and usually does not hold the viewer's attention for very long. Thus as a rule, this type of visual should be avoided in classroom displays. Informal balance, on the other hand, can be used to create visual displays that are dynamic, interesting, and compelling to the viewer. The elements in such a display are positioned on the board in a manner that is not symmetrical. A small, brightly colored object might be used to balance a larger, less colorful one.

An effective visual display is colorful but not gaudy. As a rule of thumb, it is better to use two or three coordinated colors in a display than to use four or five colors. Try using tints and shades of one color. Look at a color wheel for guidance. Colors next to each other on the wheel go well together, while those farther away are not compatible. Colors opposite each other on the wheel also go together and give the greatest contrast. Sometimes the amount of contrast is too startling, sometimes not. The best way to determine if colors go together is to place them next to each other and make your own decision. One shade of red may look good with a forest green, while another shade of red may clash. Years ago there were all sorts of rules about which colors went together. Remember when it was considered wrong to use pink with red? Colors that we would not have dreamed of using together at one time now are acceptable, even in vogue. One final word about color selection: Often the content of a display will indicate what colors should be used—for example, a Christmas display might be done in green and red; an American history board in red, white, and blue; and a display about Israel in light blue and white. Sometimes we want to use realistic colors, other times we don't. Do elephants always have to be brown or gray?

A visual must catch the viewer's attention quickly and hold it for as long as it is necessary to get the message across. Attention grabbers may assume a variety of forms. A catchy caption using a play on words or a caption that asks a question will spark interest. A moving object or a blinking light will attract attention. Giving the viewer something to do or to manipulate at the board will maintain interest. For example, you could provide the viewer with a set of questions to answer, a set of objects to match, or a group of items to move about the board.

## Eye Catchers

Bulletin boards are two-dimensional surfaces on which flat objects are displayed. Yet we experience the world in three dimensions; what we see has depth. A bulletin board display that has a three-dimensional look is unique and almost always arouses interest. As you read the descriptions that accompany each of the bulletin board ideas in this book, you will notice that they all contain three-dimensional objects. Blue jeans, T-shirts, shorts, and hats of all types clothe the people and animals in these displays. What child can resist a big, floppy bear wearing a ski cap or an elephant with a colorful bandanna around its neck?

Texture in the display is another vehicle for arousing and holding interest. It says "please touch." It is suggested that animals be constructed so that their bodies appear to be covered with fur. The most expensive way to achieve this is to purchase yards of fun fur, sometimes called fantasy fur, at a local fabric shop. Less expensive alternatives include constructing animals from second-hand fur coats, bathroom rugs with a long nap, or carpeting with a high pile. The biggest problem when using carpeting is that it is difficult to cut with a pair of ordinary scissors. Other approaches to incorporating texture into displays include making "hair" from knitting yarn, selecting papers with a variety of finishes, and using different types of fabrics. Burlap, felt, corduroy, flocked paper, vinyl, and foil wallpaper should all be considered. Be careful not to overdo it; too many different textures in a display will impair its communication value, not increase it. Moderation in the use of texture will ensure the simplicity needed for the display to be most effective.

Another technique for making displays three-dimensional is to attach baskets, boxes, and other types of containers to the board. Objects to manipulate, handouts to be taken away, and actual objects for display can be placed inside. If the container is not too deep, it may be used as is and anchored to the board with T-pins. Heavy or deep containers will need to be cut in half before being attached to the board.

Displays that include moving objects or blinking lights can also add zip to the presentation. Strings of Christmas lights or a low-watt frosted bulb placed in a flasher attachment that plugs into the wall are useful. Discarded store displays containing a small, battery-operated motor provide a source of perpetual motion. Flashing lights and continuously moving objects may distract students from attending to certain learning tasks; use these techniques with discretion.

Finally, you will notice that there are suggestions for incorporating actual objects into many of the displays in this book. Balls, toys, food, and empty containers of all types can be used. Cut bulky objects in half to facilitate securing them to the board. Extremely large objects may have to be attached inconspicuously from the ceiling with transparent fishing line. It is best to avoid displaying anything that is irreplaceable or of great value in case someone decides to remove articles from the display.

## Watching Your Pennies

As a rule, elementary schools stock some of the basic materials needed to construct bulletin board displays; most common among these are rolls of bulletin board paper in a variety of colors. Not only can this type of paper serve its intended purpose of covering the background of the display, it can also be used for cutting out letters for the caption, making borders around pictures and verbal material, constructing paper sculptures, or adding visual details to the display. In lieu of this type of paper, schools may provide rolls of corrugated paper in a variety of colors. Unfortunately, this type of paper is not as versatile as bulletin board paper and is more appropriate as borders and backgrounds. Using a variety of papers and fabrics in the display will arouse interest and help get the intended message across. Often there is little cash available to educators for purchasing expensive papers and fabrics. With a little organization, ingenuity, and time, a plentiful supply of bulletin board construction materials can be secured quite inexpensively.

At the beginning of the school year, most teachers communicate by letter with parents, outlining the goals, activities, and responsibilities that will make the year a productive and successful experience for each child in the class. At this time, or shortly thereafter, send home a list of common household items that will be needed to carry out art projects, construct self-instructional learning materials, and prepare attractive bulletin boards; request that parents contribute whatever they can. Suggest that this is an opportunity to do some housecleaning and make some extra space in closets, in cabinets, and on shelves. A parent who sews may have all sorts of fabric remnants to donate, and a knitter may have parts of skeins of yarn in a multitude of colors. Someone who has recently redecorated may have partial rolls of wallpaper left over. And almost everyone has some gift wrapping paper. If you know that you will need twelve empty cardboard boxes of the same size, make a request. Of course, it is necessary to be sensitive to the fact that some families simply are unable to help out.

Another approach is to tap community resources. Tailors, woodworkers, wallpaper hangers, carpet layers, and others may be glad to give you their scraps just for the asking. Take whatever they contribute, keep what you can use, discard what you don't need, and send a nice note to those who contribute. Local manufacturers may have items to donate, too. A paper manufacturer supplied us with roll ends of white heavy paper that came in handy for all sorts of art projects and displays. They were ours for the taking. Local merchants are constantly discarding boxes, corrugated cartons, and packing materials. If you ask, they are usually willing to let you check out their rubbish pile. You may even ask some local merchants to save display items for you.

Often books of wallpaper samples, swatches of upholstery fabric, and sets of carpet samples are yours for the asking. Paint and decorating stores in small towns will usually be glad to help you out at no cost at all. Sometimes, especially in larger cities, a small fee is charged for the samples.

Garage and rummage sales provide some of the best bargains. For as little as a dime you can purchase items of clothing to dress the figures. Odds and ends of wrapping paper, fabric, yarn, and ribbons are readily available. Don't forget toys and balls of all descriptions, too. While you are at it, used books, games, records, and puzzles for all age levels are also plentiful—an excellent way to revitalize a classroom collection of instructional materials. Before buying any of these items, check to see that they are in good condition and are complete. More expensive sources of merchandise include thrift shops, flea markets, auctions, and outlet stores.

One of the aims of using secondhand items or discards is to save energy and natural resources by recycling. Ask tennis instructors to keep dead balls for you, painters and artists not to discard their old brushes, parents to save outgrown children's clothing, or youngsters to lend you a toy now and then. Believe it or not, some people have found all types of new or nearly new items in apartment complex dumpsters, especially around the end of the month when leases are up and people move. It is unbelievable that on Christmas day, one can find rolls of brand new gift wrap in the trash. Ecologically, this is a serious waste. Save a tree, check the trash.

A substantial amount has been written about sources of sponsored instructional materials that can be obtained for the asking. Pamphlets, charts, maps, and posters from businesses and industries; professional organizations and societies; local, state, and foreign governments; and social service organizations are welcome additions to one's collection of instructional materials. Obtain these by writing letters on school stationery or by making toll-free phone calls. Keep your eyes open for free offers in magazines and professional journals.

## Tools and Procedures

The proper tools get a job done as easily as possible. When it comes to gathering the necessary supplies and equipment to construct a bulletin board display, nothing sophisticated, unique, or exotic is required. The following will help you get started:

pair of sturdy, sharp scissors
sharp single-edged razor blade in holder
no. 2 pencil
art gum eraser
permanent wide-tipped felt markers (black, red, blue, green)
white glue
rubber cement
white chalk
straight pins with plain heads
T-pins
thumb tacks
stapler that opens
staples
nylon fishing line
18-inch metal ruler
yard stick
ball of string
opaque projector
drymount press
drymount tissue
laminating film
paper cutter
die-cut cardboard letters

All the displays in this book may be reproduced easily with the aid of an opaque projector. The size of the display surface you wish to cover will determine how large the components of the display will have to be. Trace images onto light-colored paper or fabric with a pencil; on dark surfaces trace with white chalk. Generally speaking, if you are going to dress figures in real clothing, reproduce only the parts of the body that are visible, such as hands, feet, and faces.

If pictures or pages of reading material are part of the display, place a uniform ¼-inch to ½-inch border around each one to give them a neat, finished look. By far, the best way to mount items permanently is to use the dry-mounting process. Follow instructions provided by the manufacturer of the drymount tissue or those found in any audiovisual production book. The easiest way to ensure that the borders are uniform is to use a mount board that is 2 to 3 inches longer and wider than the items being mounted. Precise measurement of the mount board and centering of the display item are not essential. After the mount is removed from the press and cooled, mark the desired width of the border at intervals all the way around the display item. Connect these marks with a light pencil line. Trim along these four lines with a paper cutter and you have a uniform border.

One temporary mounting method involves evenly spreading rubber cement on the back of the display item, positioning the item on colored paper or posterboard, and then trimming off the excess border in the same manner as described above. Avoid using white glue since it usually produces lumpy, bumpy results. White glue is best for adhering fabric to cardboard or fabric to fabric. A less permanent method of bordering is to cut four thin strips of colored paper and to attach these in such a way as to form a "picture frame" around the item being displayed. This method has its drawbacks. Each time the item is attached to the display surface, the border must be positioned all over again. Another way to prepare temporary borders is to center and pin the item to be mounted on a sheet of colored paper that is ½-inch to 1-inch longer and wider than the item itself.

All elements in a display must be visible and must contrast well with the colors around them. With few exceptions, colored chalks and crayons should be avoided because they are not dark or bold enough to be seen from a distance. Permanent markers, those that are not water soluble, are darker and thus more visible. Before laminating surfaces on which these markers are used, dry the item in a drymount press or with an iron to prevent bleeding. Avoid coloring in large areas with markers because the results will be full of streaks. Instead, affix colored paper to these large areas using rubber cement.

Any display item that will be handled repeatedly by the viewer should be laminated to increase its durability. Unless both sides of lightweight materials are laminated, they will curl and be very difficult to handle or display. Surfaces that need to be marked on repeatedly can have

an extended life if they are laminated and then marked on with a temporary transparency marker or grease pencil. Laminating is also used to make the colors in papers or pictures appear brighter.

Attach items to the display surface in the least conspicuous way possible. The shiny heads of thumbtacks or the brightly colored tops of push pins should be kept out of sight because they tend to clutter the display and detract from the visual message. Straight pins and staples are the least noticeable means of attaching objects to the board and should be used whenever possible. Of course, thumbtacks often are needed to support heavy objects, but keep them out of sight. T-pins support heavy objects well, too.

## Letter Perfect

Producing legible, attractive captions for instructional displays need not be difficult. Remembering that the aim of this book is to help you create motivational displays that are simple and attractive, there is no need to explore all the ways that exist for producing captions. However, three methods warrant some discussion here.

The most costly of these involves purchasing commercially produced cardboard letters that can either be used as is or painted to fit the board's color scheme. Each time you need a new color for a new display, it will be necessary to purchase a new set of letters or to repaint those you have. This method is neither cost-effective nor practical.

An alternative is to purchase a set of plastic pin-backed letters. Usually these come in black or white, which does not permit you to coordinate the color of your caption with the colors in the display, but they may be painted a limited number of times.

By far, the most practical method is to purchase one set of 3- to 4-inch heavy cardboard letters for making major captions and one set of 2-inch die-cut letters for identifying labels and to use these as tracing patterns. By doing this, the color scheme may be maintained easily, captions may be saved for repeated use, and the cost will be kept to the initial investment of two sets of letters. Many school supply stores sell die-cut cardboard letters by the piece; others sell them in sets. The latter can be quite expensive because a set usually consists of many of the same letter. If children are just learning to read and write, both upper and lower case letters should appear in the display so as not to cause confusion. Use all capital letters for audiences of older children and adults.

When used as patterns, die-cut letters give you the flexibility to make captions from all sorts of paper, a variety of fabrics, and even wood. When tracing letters, place them upside down on the back of the fabric or paper to be used. Trace them with a pencil, being sure to reproduce each letter with truly straight lines or true curves. With a sharp pair of scissors, cut along the pencil guidelines. Cut away from corners with a sharp single-edge razor blade. It may be necessary to cut through the letter in an inconspicuous place to reach the inside of letters such as "B" and "R." When you turn the cutout letter over, the pencil marks will not show, so there is no need to erase. If you are going to drymount or laminate letters, do this *before* cutting them out. Unless the paper is very heavy, both sides of the letters will need to be laminated to prevent curling.

One of the limitations of using the same letter pattern over and over is that it can become monotonous. This need not be the case. Variety can be achieved by avoiding the repeated use of solid colors. Consider making letters from patterned papers and fabrics, newspapers, maps, vinyl, and textured wallpapers. Fabric letters will have body and be easy to handle and display if the fabric is drymounted to lightweight cardboard before tracing and cutting takes place. Because many synthetic fabrics melt in the drymount press, it is necessary to test a little piece of the cloth in the press before proceeding. Fabrics that have a high cotton content will not melt. Vinyl papers may melt, so always test them first. To give lettering the appearance of depth, cut two sets of identical captions, making one of the sets from a solid dark or light color. When attaching these to the display, offset the solid letters a little to the right of the top set, thus achieving a shadow effect. Attaching cutout letters to the board with straight pins and then pulling them out to the heads of the pins will produce a three-dimensional look.

No matter how attractive letters are, they will not serve their purpose unless they are attached to the board in straight lines and are spaced appropriately. Since we read from left to right in our society, captions and labels should be placed horizontally on the board. Avoid hard-to-read vertical or diagonal placement. To ensure that the letters will be straight, use a yardstick as a guide or attach a string where you want the bottom of the letters to rest and use this as a guide. Once you are satisfied, remove the string. Whenever possible, place the entire caption at the top or at the bottom of the display. This is easier to read than a message that is separated into parts.

Lettering will be legible if careful attention is given to spacing. Within words, letters should appear to be equally spaced. The only way to achieve this is to move the letters around until the spaces between them appear to be equal. Since letters are of varying widths, measuring will not work. Spacing between words should also appear to be equal so that groups of letters form distinct units. Leave sufficient space between lines of words and be careful not to crowd them to the border of the display surface. Too much or too little space between letters, words, and lines will confuse the message and make it difficult to read.

## In Conclusion

Now it's time to try out some of the ideas that appear on the following pages. The information that accompanies each illustration is merely intended to serve as a guide to assist you in the preparation of attractive bulletin boards. Materials and color suggestions are just that. You may wish to deviate from these if you feel you have a better idea, can think of an easier way of doing something, or do not have access to the suggested materials. In some cases, the idea provided may not be appropriate for your classroom, but with a few changes it could be made to work for you. Go right ahead, remembering that the purpose of these displays is to arouse student interest through the liberal use of three-dimensional objects. Get out the opaque or overhead projector, gather up your tools and materials, and go for it!

**SUBJECT AREA:**   Language arts.

**PURPOSE:**   To introduce homonyms.

**MONEY SAVER:**   The rabbit may be made out of a burlap sack or a remnant of light gray fabric.

**ADDING DIMENSIONALITY:**   Stuff the rabbit's head, especially the cheeks. One ear should be floppy and should hang out from the board. Place wire in the ear to accomplish this. Whiskers are made from heavy pipe cleaners.

**COLOR SCHEME:**   Border = dark purple; background = orchid; hills = magenta or fuchsia; hair = pink; rabbit = brown or gray; bow tie = stripes or polka dots in bright coordinated colors; fence = white; lettering = dark purple.

**CONSTRUCTION HINTS:**   For hair, use large quantities of pink cellophane Easter grass or excelsior; import/export stores, for example, often receive breakable merchandise packed in the latter. To make a bow tie that will not droop, gather a rectangle of stiff or starched fabric at its center. With a pointed object (e.g., a drawing compass), bore small holes in one length of the wooden garden fence. Place straight pins in the holes to securely fasten the fence to the board. Screw two ⅞-inch cup hooks into the fence.

**CONTENT HINTS:**   Prepare a set of circles for an activity in which students match homonym pairs. Laminate both sides of circles on which homonyms are written. Punch a hole in each so it can be hung on the cup hook. Make the activity self-checking. If the display is used at Easter, substitute colorful eggs for circles.

**ADAPTATIONS:**   (1) Change the caption to "Funny Bunny." On circles place rhyming words for students to match. (2) Compound words may be learned in the same way. Use the caption "Cotton + Tail = Cottontail." Make both of these activities self-checking by placing appropriate answers on the back of the circles. (3) Use as a story-starter board. In place of the fence, attach flexible straw baskets filled with bouquets of paper or fabric flowers and change the caption to "When Spring Comes . . ."

**ZIP MOVES THE MAIL**

**SUBJECT AREA:**   Language arts.

**PURPOSE:**   To demonstrate why zip codes are needed on letters and packages sent through the U.S. mail.

**MONEY SAVER:**   From your mail and that of friends, save envelopes and mailers that have cancelled stamps and contain zip codes. Collect road maps for the background of the display.

**ADDING DIMENSIONALITY:**   Fill the postal carrier's bag with mail and place a few letters in his hand.

**COLOR SCHEME:**   Border = black; background = red, white, blue; clothing = blue; face and hands = pink; lettering = red; postal bag, details = black; envelope = white.

**CONSTRUCTION HINTS:**   Cover the board with maps that have been trimmed so that only the map portion remains. With permanent markers, duplicate a postage stamp on a sheet of white poster board. Draw black

lines where the address and return address are located. Laminate and trim to appropriate size. Border the envelope in red or blue. Address the envelope with black temporary transparency marker; *do not* use a permanent marker. Carrier's bag may be made of cloth or paper.

**CONTENT HINTS:**   Some of the mail should contain stamps from foreign countries or U.S. stamps that depict a variety of cultures. Children may take turns addressing the large envelope. Temporary marker can be removed easily with a damp cloth.

**ADAPTATIONS:**   (1) Change the caption to "From Me to You" and use as a motivator for a letter-writing unit. (2) Change the caption to "Where, Oh, Where?" and replace the envelope with a mounted map of the U.S. surrounded by envelopes addressed to individuals in U.S. cities. Using pieces of yarn, connect the envelopes to their corresponding locations on the map. (3) Use this idea again, this time displaying a world map and envelopes addressed to people in a number of foreign countries.

**SUBJECT AREA:**   Language arts.

**PURPOSE:**   To introduce or reinforce the initial "m" sound.

**MONEY SAVER:**   Collect everyday objects that begin with "m." You may wish to ask students to contribute or lend items for display.

**ADDING DIMENSIONALITY:**   The monkey is a stuffed toy. The M&M's and mittens are real objects. The mouse tails and whiskers are made from pipe cleaners.

**COLOR SCHEME:**   Border = black; background = light blue; mice = brown and white; mailbox = white, orange flag, brown post; lettering = orange (m), yellow (M).

**CONSTRUCTION HINTS:**   Give letters the illusion of depth. Out of black paper cut one lowercase "m" and one uppercase "M" that are equal in size to the orange and yellow "m"s. Offset each colored letter by placing it on top of its black counterpart so that the black appears to be a shadow. Both the mailbox and mice are made from colored paper.

**CONTENT HINTS:**   Let your imagination be your guide in selecting "m" objects to include in this display. You need not be bound by what is illustrated here.

**ADAPTATIONS:**   Portray other consonants, long and short vowels, or consonant blends in the same manner. This display is appropriate for bilingual, monolingual, and foreign language instruction.

**SUBJECT AREA:** Language arts.

**PURPOSE:** To reinforce the need to use rough drafts when writing.

**MONEY SAVER:** For the tree branch, locate a page of wood-grain vinyl wallpaper in a sample book. Real leaves may be used, if they are dried first.

**ADDING DIMENSIONALITY:** For greatest interest, make the owl's feathers from strips of silver and black paper. Cut one edge of each strip in a zigzag fashion. Attach the strips in alternating layers on a cardboard form that has been cut into the shape of an owl. Alternately, the owl can be made out of shag carpeting or a bathroom rug.

**COLOR SCHEME:** Border = black; background = light blue; writing sample mounts = orange; owl = black and silver; feet and leaves = orange; pencil = yellow with orange eraser; lettering = black.

**CONSTRUCTION HINTS:** Make the pencil from rolled paper, make a cone for the tip, and use contrasting rolled paper for the eraser. Felt or paper is used to form the owl's eyes. Both the tree branch on which the owl is sitting and the leaves at its feet are made from paper, but both may be real.

**CONTENT HINTS:** Writing examples should include a first draft with corrections, a revision, and a final product. Border each of these with orange paper or poster board.

**ADAPTATIONS:** (1) Change the caption to "Be Wise . . . Analyze" and include verbal, numerical, or visual problem-solving activities where the drafts are located (provide answers), (2) Change the caption to "Be Wise . . . Organize" and in place of drafts, position cutout letters and numbers that show correct outline form, (3) Change the caption to "Give a Hoot" and replace drafts with mounted news items that describe people helping others.

**SUBJECT AREA:** Language arts.

**PURPOSE:** To provide practice in reading, research, and problem solving.

**MONEY SAVER:** This is an inexpensive board because it can be made of scraps of paper and fabric.

**ADDING DIMENSIONALITY:** Visualization is accomplished by placing a real object or an object constructed from fabric next to each question.

**COLOR SCHEME:** Border = light blue; background = yellow; objects = variable, mostly greens and browns; rows = light blue; lettering = light blue.

**CONSTRUCTION HINTS:** Questions are displayed on cards that are opened to reveal the correct answer. Fold 5″ × 8″ white, unlined index cards in half to a size of 5″ × 4″. On the outside of each card, neatly type, print, or write each question. In the same manner, place the answer under the flap formed.

**CONTENT HINTS:** Relate questions to a unit of study in progress. As a language arts activity, have students use research and writing skills to prepare questions for display. Accompany questions with appropriate visual material.

**ADAPTATIONS:** By replacing the questions and visual material with a series of small, mounted pictures, the layout of this board can serve as a skeleton for any number of displays. To achieve a three-dimensional effect, pull the pictures out from board to the heads of straight pins. To aid in communicating the message, label each picture. Here's an excellent way to arouse interest in geography or in famous males and females of varying cultural backgrounds. Change the caption to "Monkey Business," pin mounted pictures of different types of simians along the blue strips, and you have a motivating science display.

**KNOWLEDGE HAS NO LIMITS**

**SUBJECT AREA:** Reading.

**PURPOSE:** To arouse interest in content area reading.

**MONEY SAVER:** Borrow a lightweight protective suit from the fire department or a local laboratory. A jumpsuit may be used as a substitute.

**ADDING DIMENSIONALITY:** Books are made from cardboard boxes that are covered with colorful paper. Cake mix or cereal boxes work well. To form antennae, attach styrofoam balls to the end of heavy pipe cleaners or long springs. Actual ski mittens and winter boots add realism to the display.

**COLOR SCHEME:** Border = black; background = light blue; space suit = yellow; helmet = orange; gloves and boots = black with blue stripes; stars = silver; lettering = yellow.

**CONSTRUCTION HINTS:** Coordinate the lettering on "books" with the color of each cover. Combinations that work well include: yellow and orange, green and yellow, blue and orange, red and pink, brown and yellow.

**CONTENT HINTS:** Label each "book" with the name of a curricular area (e.g., science, math, English, etc.).

**ADAPTATIONS:** (1) This board can be modified for use in all subject areas. Modify the caption to read "Science Has No Limits," and on the "book" covers place mounted magazine pictures that illustrate the theme of the board. (2) Change the caption to "Spaced Out" and display information about space exploration or astronomy on the "book" covers. (3) Change the caption to "Fly Me to the Moon" and display mounted pictures and verbal information about the moon.

**SUBJECT AREA:**   Reading.

**PURPOSE:**   To promote an interest in reading.

**MONEY SAVER:**   Borrow book jackets from the school library media specialist. Use a piece of rope that is about ¾″ in diameter for pulling the wagon.

**ADDING DIMENSIONALITY:**   Place book jackets in the wagon. Use pipe cleaners for the bunny's whiskers and a yarn pompom or fuzzy ball for its tail. If desired, the wagon may be made from a corrugated box. Fringe green paper for grass.

**COLOR SCHEME:**   Border = dark green; background = yellow; bunny = white; wagon = brown; lettering = dark green.

**CONSTRUCTION HINTS:**   Brightly colored fabric makes the bunny's jacket attractive. Dots on the bunny's cheeks are red and features are black.

**CONTENT HINTS:**   Spring is the best time of year for displaying this board. Books represented should be written by or about males and females of various ethnic origins.

**ADAPTATIONS:**   (1) Replace book jackets with laminated Easter eggs on which are placed self-checking reading activities. (2) Change the caption to "Hop to It . . . Write" and replace book jackets with laminated eggs that have story starters on them. (3) Change the caption to "Robert Rabbit Says . . ." and have children write something positive about a classmate; then place their comments in the wagon. Once a week set aside a time to share these thoughts. Monitor comments so that no one is slighted or embarrassed.

# READING IS MMM GOOD

**SUBJECT AREA:** Reading.

**PURPOSE:** To encourage students to explore books.

**MONEY SAVER:** From the school library media specialist borrow the jackets from books written by males and females who represent diverse cultural backgrounds.

**ADDING DIMENSIONALITY:** To form the soup can, cover half of a cylindrical cardboard or plastic packing container with colored paper. Use a real spoon and napkin.

**COLOR SCHEME:** Border = red; background = yellow; can = red and white; bowl = red with yellow stripes; napkin = red; lettering = red, M-M-M = black.

**CONSTRUCTION HINTS:** The bowl may be either a pocket made of felt or a round container that has been cut in half and mounted to look like a bowl. It needs to be sturdy enough to hold book jackets.

**CONTENT HINTS:** On the soup can replace the name "SMITH" with your name. Select books that relate to individual student interests or to a specific unit of study. If possible, have the books shown in the display available in your classroom for students to read.

**ADAPTATIONS:** (1) Change the caption to "M-M-M Good" and place recipes in the bowl for classroom reading and cooking—good practice in following directions. (2) Place menus or recipes in the bowl along with laminated activity cards that call on students to use reading comprehension and/or math skills. Activities should require students to use the information contained in the menus and recipes. (3) Make this a content reading board. As an example, change the caption to "Science Is M-M-M Good" and in the bowl place book jackets, magazines, and pamphlets that deal with science.

**SUBJECT AREA:**   Reading.

**PURPOSE:**   To promote reading interest.

**MONEY SAVER:**   Borrow book jackets from your library. Obtain broken fruit baskets from a local grocer.

**ADDING DIMENSIONALITY:**   Attach a wicker basket or a fruit basket that has been cut in half to the bulletin board. Make the giraffe's horns from xylophone sticks or a pair of large knitting needles. Use yarn or paper strips for the mane and tail.

**COLOR SCHEME:**   Border = brown; background = yellow; giraffe = orange and black; lettering = orange.

**CONSTRUCTION HINTS:**   Have students make leaves or collect and preserve real ones. Avoid placing all the book jackets flat against the board. For realism, make the giraffe out of fuzzy fabric. Curly paper eyelashes give the giraffe added personality.

**CONTENT HINTS:**   Select book jackets that represent authors and writings from various cultures. If possible, focus on a different theme each week (e.g., sports, animals, spring) and display book jackets that relate to these themes. Encourage in-class reading by having the books featured in the display available in the classroom reading center. Change jackets frequently.

**ADAPTATIONS:**   (1) Use as a book report board by having students make illustrated book jackets of books they've read. (2) Change the caption to "Take Your Pick . . . Write!" and have students write stories or poems on leaf-shaped paper. Place these on leaves that are the same shape but that are cut a little larger. Vary the color of leaves with the season of the year. (3) Make a getting-to-know-you display to start off the school year. Change the caption to "Our Gang." Omit the book jackets. Place a student's name on each leaf. If necessary, fill the branches with additional leaves.

**DON'T BE AN ALIEN TO BOOKS**

**SUBJECT AREA:** Reading.

**PURPOSE:** To promote an interest in recreational reading.

**MONEY SAVER:** Locate a fabric remnant or feathers for making the bird's body.

**ADDING DIMENSIONALITY:** The creature on the right is made from cotton balls. A plastic fish bowl cut in half makes a good space helmet for the bird. The bird's beak is constructed from pieces of orange cardboard that are attached so they stick out from the board. The space creature has jiggly craft eyes.

**COLOR SCHEME:** Border = green; background = yellow planet, blue sky; bird = yellow with orange feet; space creature = green; surface creatures = orange; lettering = yellow.

**CONSTRUCTION HINTS:** Construct the bird's body using feathers, long fun fur, or a fabric remnant. Cut a piece of cardboard in the shape of the space creature, and to this glue cotton balls that have been colored with green chalk. Craters drawn with a black permanent marker on a semicircle of paper make a realistic-looking "planet" for the creatures to stand on.

**CONTENT HINTS:** Let children create their own creatures and place the title of a book they have read on each creature. Display creatures on the planet's surface and on the walls surrounding the bulletin board.

**ADAPTATIONS:** "Science Is Out of This World" or "Math Is Out of This World" are both captions that could be substituted for the one originally suggested. Or, change the caption to "It's Out of This World" and use the display to help introduce a unit on figures of speech. Have students identify other figures of speech, write them on ameoba-shaped forms, and tack them on the planet's surface.

**CUDDLE UP WITH A FRIEND**

**SUBJECT AREA:** Reading.

**PURPOSE:** To arouse interest is reading.

**MONEY SAVER:** The cat is wearing a real ski cap and is reading a paperback book or magazine. An old fur coat or fuzzy bathrobe makes an appealing animal. A used oval rag rug or throw rug becomes a comfortable resting place.

**ADDING DIMENSIONALITY:** If you don't use a coat to construct the cat, make it from layers of quilted material covered with fun fur. Strips of wood make the window frame look real. To the board, attach a light-weight paperback book or the cover, back, and a few pages from a magazine so reading material appears to be standing upright in front of cat.

**COLOR SCHEME:** Border = medium green; background = light blue; cat = brown, black, white, or gray; rug and books = multicolored; lettering = medium green.

**CONSTRUCTION HINTS:** The ski cap should be colorful, even whimsical. The cat's facial features must contrast well enough with the fur to be easily distinguished. To form the window, glue strips of wood, wood grain wallpaper or shelf liner, or brown paper on top of a winter scene that has been covered with cellophane or laminating film. Children can prepare this scene using tempera paint or chalks, or it may be a paper collage.

**CONTENT HINTS:** The book or magazine the cat is reading should be selected carefully to spark student interest.

**ADAPTATIONS:** Omit the books and window. Replace the ski cap with a straw hat or baseball cap. To the background of the display, attach pastel-colored paper daisies. On the petals place (1) pairs of synonyms, antonyms, or homonyms; (2) examples of one of the parts of speech; or (3) fractions, math facts, or decimals. Change caption to "Dreaming of . . . ," inserting the appropriate word in the blank. For example, use the caption "Dreaming of Antonyms" and place word pairs such as "hard—soft" on each petal. Children should be encouraged to help make the flowers.

**IT'S IN THE BAG**

**SUBJECT AREA:** Reading.

**PURPOSE:** To provide reading practice.

**MONEY SAVER:** Ask the school custodian for a plastic trash bag for the bird to hold.

**ADDING DIMENSIONALITY:** Stuff the bag with crumpled newspaper so it looks partially full.

**COLOR SCHEME:** Border = red; background = light blue; bird = yellow with orange feet and beak; pocket = yellow; lettering = red.

**CONSTRUCTION HINTS:** Put a false bottom in the bag so that the objects students put in it can be removed easily. If feathers or long-napped fun fur are not available, make the bird out of paper. The pocket can be made from felt or heavy cotton fabric.

**CONTENT HINTS:** Write sight recognition words on cards, laminate, and place in the pocket. Have a child pick a word from the pocket and read it aloud. If the child is correct, the card is placed in the trash bag. Use as a teacher-led, small-group activity or one in which the children work together to fill the bag.

**ADAPTATIONS:** Variations are endless. Cards may contain math facts, social studies or science questions, spelling words for the week, or vocabulary words. When appropriate, place answers on the back of the cards for self-checking.

# SAIL INTO READING

**SUBJECT AREA:** Reading.

**PURPOSE:** To promote an interest in recreational reading.

**MONEY SAVER:** Fill the sailboat with book jackets and magazines you have borrowed from your library media specialist.

**ADDING DIMENSIONALITY:** Drape the fabric sails. For extra firmness, starch the sails or make them from a stiff material. Loop real rope on the boat hull and masts. Masts can be made from wooden dowels.

**COLOR SCHEME:** Border = light blue; boat = orange; sails and clouds = white; waves = dark blue; water and sky = light blue; lettering = orange.

**CONSTRUCTION HINTS:** Make the anchor from gold foil paper or wallpaper. Extend the masts into the top border or just above the top edge of the bulletin board. Staple the sails to the mast so the staples do not show.

**CONTENT HINTS:** Reading materials should be written by and about males and females from different ethnic backgrounds.

**ADAPTATIONS:** (1) Use as a content reading display by employing the caption "Sail into Geography" or "Sail into Science" and fill the boat with corresponding reading material. (2) Change the caption to "Sail into Literature" and replace the book jackets and magazines with boxes that are covered with different colored paper. Label each "book" with words like poetry, essay, biography, fiction. (3) Change the caption to "Nautical Nines" and using the box idea again, present on each "book" math facts that describe the number nine. By changing the caption and facts, any number can be illustrated.

**SUBJECT AREA:** Math.

**PURPOSE:** To present different ways of obtaining the same number.

**MONEY SAVER:** Use fabric remnants to clothe the witch and to construct ghosts.

**ADDING DIMENSIONALITY:** Drape the witch in black cloth and make her hair out of orange yarn. Fire can be made using red and orange cellophane. A black dowel can be used to stir witch's brew.

**COLOR SCHEME:** Border = black; background = light blue; witch = orange face; numbers = orange; plus and equal signs = black; lettering = black.

**CONSTRUCTION HINTS:** All the figures can be made from colored paper, but they will be much more enticing if they are three-dimensional. Angel hair can be used to make the ghosts. Use a rubber or plastic spider web and spider(s).

**CONTENT HINTS:** This board is particularly effective around Halloween. The math facts can be changed as needed. If appropriate, include subtraction, multiplication, or division problems. Whole numbers and fractions may appear in problems for older students. Problems may be arranged vertically and/or horizontally. Have students make up problems to solve.

**ADAPTATIONS:** Change the caption to "What's Cooking?" Where the math problems were, attach little cauldrons containing recipes. A copy of the recipe should be attached to the outside of each cauldron. (1) Use recipes for handwriting, language, or additional math activities. (2) Select recipes that can be prepared in the classroom; design activities that involve reading, measuring, following directions, and eating. (3) During October, use the caption "Bewitching Papers," omit the math problems, and display student work. Change the board daily. Display each child's work at least once during the month.

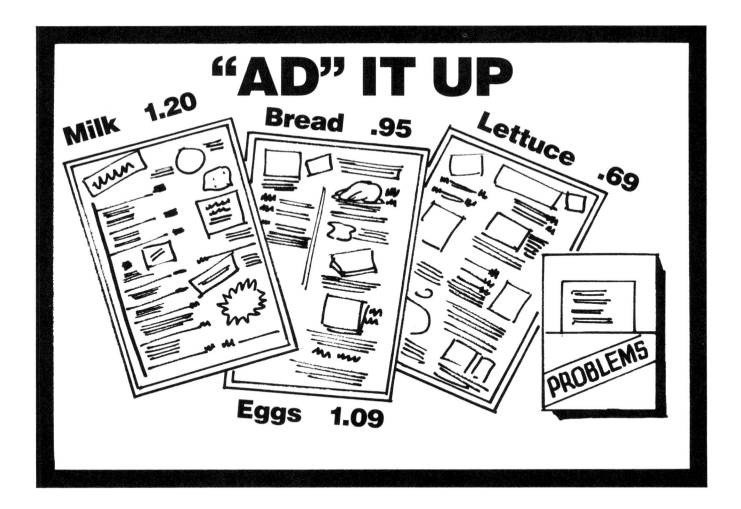

**SUBJECT AREA:** Math.

**PURPOSE:** To provide practice in solving story problems.

**MONEY SAVER:** Use food ad pages from your local newspaper.

**ADDING DIMENSIONALITY:** Attach a pocket or container to the board. Fill it with laminated cards containing problems that relate to the newspaper pages displayed. Attach the caption to the board with straight pins and pull the letters and symbols in "AD" to the head of the pins.

**COLOR SCHEME:** Border = red; background = black; lettering = white, "AD" = red and white.

**CONSTRUCTION HINTS:** Shadow the word "AD" by placing a set of white letters under the red ones. Create a ½″ border for each newspaper page by mounting them on red sheets of paper or poster board. For durability, laminate the newspaper pages.

**CONTENT HINTS:** Prepare story problems that relate to the ads displayed. Provide an answer sheet so students can check their solutions. This board is especially appropriate for a learning center. Keep the prices displayed on the board current.

**ADAPTATIONS:** (1) Use other types of ads (e.g., clothing, furniture, want ads) and develop a set of problems that relate to them. (2) Substitute menus from local restaurants for ads and prepare corresponding problems; change "AD" to "ADD." (3) Using the new caption again, substitute pages from a toy catalog for the newspaper pages and replace the names and prices of foods with those of toys. Prepare math story problems based on the catalog information displayed. For each of these adaptations, supply an answer sheet for students to check their responses.

**SUBJECT AREA:**   Math.

**PURPOSE:**   To introduce metric terms.

**MONEY SAVER:**   An old black graduation gown makes an excellent magician's robe.

**ADDING DIMENSIONALITY:**   Drape the robe. The magician's hat should be made to droop at its tip. The whiskers and eyebrows can be made from cotton batting. Slippers, which are made from the same black fabric as the hat, should be stuffed with tissue paper.

**COLOR SCHEME:**   Border = yellow; background = light blue; lightning = silver; cauldron = black with yellow symbols; lettering = yellow.

**CONSTRUCTION HINTS:**   Cut lightning bolts from cardboard and cover them with aluminum foil; or construct the bolts from silver gift wrapping paper. Use straight pins to drape the gown. Most of the pins can be hidden behind Merlin's beard. The cauldron can be made out of paper.

**CONTENT HINTS:**   October is a perfect month for this board. Place metric terms on the lightning bolts and metric abbreviations in the cauldron.

**ADAPTATIONS:**   (1) For a series of language arts displays, change the caption to "Merlin's Magic . . ." (Abbreviations, Spelling, Homonyms, Synonyms, etc.) and place appropriate words in the cauldron and on the bolts. (2) Change the caption to "Magic Money" and place cards containing actual coins and bills on the front and in the cauldron. Label each coin and bill with its name or denomination. (3) Change the caption to "Curious Crawlers" and position mounted and labeled pictures of spiders around the cauldron.

**IT ALL COMPUTES . . . TRY IT**

**SUBJECT AREA:**   Math.

**PURPOSE:**   To promote computer literacy.

**MONEY SAVER:**   Obtain used printer paper and punch cards from your school's main office, computer classes in your community, local businesses, or computer centers. Clothing can be castoffs or purchased inexpensively at thrift shops or garage sales.

**ADDING DIMENSIONALITY:**   Computer printer paper can be curled to make hair. Use a cardboard box for the head and body. Clothing, gloves, and shoes should be real.

**COLOR SCHEME:**   Border = green; background = yellow; computer = yellow with green details; clothing = blue jeans, red and blue plaid shirt, red gloves; lettering = green.

**CONSTRUCTION HINTS:**   The caption will look best if computer-style lettering is used. Other simple lettering styles may be substituted. Clothing may be stuffed, if desired. A keyboard can be made using letter stickers or can be hand drawn.

**CONTENT HINTS:**   Use this board as a motivator and be sure to include computer terms on the punch cards. See suggestions below for making the display work for you.

**ADAPTATIONS:**   (1) Place the computer assignment for the day or floppy disks/cassette tapes to be used by students in the computer's "hands." (2) Remove the facial features and post a schedule of the day's computer users on the screen. (3) Display rules for computer use or a list of Logo or BASIC commands in the screen area.

# IS MATH IMPORTANT?

**SUBJECT AREA:**　Math.

**PURPOSE:**　To portray daily applications of mathematics.

**MONEY SAVER:**　Attach the empty case of a broken calculator to the table top. Locate a blouse or T-shirt that will complement the other colors in the display (i.e., yellow, white, red). Collect bills, forms, and receipts for display.

**ADDING DIMENSIONALITY:**　Make hair from yarn or use a short wig. Attach a real pencil to the table.

**COLOR SCHEME:**　Border = white; background = light blue; table = brown; lettering = dark blue.

**CONSTRUCTION HINTS:**　Most of the elements in this display can be made using colored paper. Skin color is brown or beige.

**CONTENT HINTS:**　Mount a 1040 EZ income tax form, cash register tapes, a bank statement, and cancelled checks on a dark blue background, being sure to leave a ¼″ to ½″ border around each. The sheet of paper on the table contains calculations.

**ADAPTATIONS:**　(1) Change the caption to "Tricky Triangles" and replace the calculator and sheet of calculations with a geometric drawing containing many triangles. Run a contest in which students identify the types or number of triangles found. (2) Change the caption to "Puzzling!"; omit the calculator and sheet of calculations and post brain teasers, cryptograms, riddles, or visual puzzles for students to solve. Provide answers. Students may want to contribute puzzles for display. (3) Change the caption to "Did You Remember?" and at the beginning of the year, display a large mounted example of a properly headed paper.

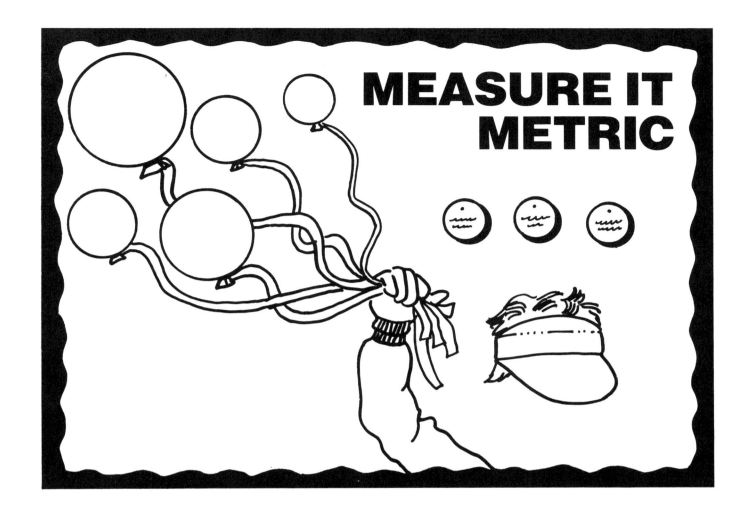

# MEASURE IT METRIC

**SUBJECT AREA:** Math.

**PURPOSE:** To provide practice in linear metric measurement.

**MONEY SAVER:** Obtain a curly wig, a sun visor, and gardening gloves from your free and inexpensive sources.

**ADDING DIMENSIONALITY:** For each balloon, sew two circular pieces of fabric (preferably satin) together, stuff them, gather at the bottom, and attach matching ribbons that will serve as balloon strings. Attach the wig, visor, and gloves to the board as shown in the illustration.

**COLOR SCHEME:** Border = pink; background = light brown; balloons = pink, red, blue, purple; lettering = pink.

**CONSTRUCTION HINTS:** Vary the size of the balloons and the length of the ribbons (strings). Construct a sleeve by draping and attaching a tube of fabric to the board with straight pins. Provide a wooden meter stick for measuring. Drape balloon strings through the gloved hand; do not pin them onto the hand.

**CONTENT HINTS:** Below the caption, post laminated circles presenting problems that relate to objects on the board (e.g., longest balloon string, size of balloons, sleeve length). Place the answers to the problems on the back of each circle for self-checking. Change the problems as needed. If desired, color code the circles according to level of difficulty. This is a good learning center activity.

**ADAPTATIONS:** (1) Change the caption to "Up, Up, and Away" and place story starters on circles. (2) Change the caption to "A Handful of Homonyms" and place homonym pairs on the balloons (read/red, blue/blew, night/knight, sore/soar) and on the front and back of the circles. (3) Change the caption to "Welcome Spring," substitute large flowers for balloons, and omit circles on which problems are written.

# BIRDS I HAVE SEEN

**SUBJECT AREA:** Science.

**PURPOSE:** To provide a system for recording observed scientific data.

**MONEY SAVER:** Dress the girl in secondhand clothing. Borrow a pair of child's binoculars. Collect real feathers that birds have shed.

**ADDING DIMENSIONALITY:** Roll brown paper into a cylinder or cover a cardboard tube with wood grain paper to form the log on which the girl is sitting. Use a black, curly wig for the hair and add a decorative bow. Next to the log, place a real knapsack containing a bird identification book.

**COLOR SCHEME:** Border = blue; background = yellow; clothing = blue jeans and white or red shirt; knapsack = red or blue; sign and log = brown; birds = various colors; lettering = blue.

**CONSTRUCTION HINTS:** If real binoculars are unavailable, make a pair from paper towel or toilet tissue tubes, painting them black and using clear cellophane for the lenses. Construct a sign holder using wood or wood grain wallpaper or shelf covering. Cut birds from paper, but place a few real feathers on their tails or wings.

**CONTENT HINTS:** On the signboard, place a beige chart that contains columns where students can record their names, the date of the sighting, the name of the bird, where it was sighted, its colors and markings, and its size. Use a black permanent marker to make the chart and then laminate it on both sides. Depending on your situation, "sightings" may be taken individually, on field trips, from films and filmstrips, or from reading materials. Student observations should be recorded on the chart using a temporary transparency marker so that old information can be removed and new data entered.

**ADAPTATIONS:** By changing the categories on the chart, a word in the caption, and the creatures in the scene, this display may be used to record information about flowers, trees, insects, reptiles, or amphibians.

# PATTERNS IN THE SKY

**SUBJECT AREA:** Science.

**PURPOSE:** To arouse interest in and reinforce knowledge of constellations.

**MONEY SAVER:** An old plush bathrobe makes a fuzzy bear, as do shaggy throw rugs.

**ADDING DIMENSIONALITY:** Pull stars to the head of T-pins so they appear to stick out from the board. Make a fluffy cloud from fiber fill or cotton batting.

**COLOR SCHEME:** Border = yellow; background = black; cloud = white; bear = yellow with white belly and face; stars = white or silver; lettering = yellow.

**CONSTRUCTION HINTS:** Trace stars on sheets of sturdy white paper or silver-colored wallpaper. Laminate both sides. Wind white rug yarn around the pins to form outlines of constellations.

**CONTENT HINTS:** Display constellations that are appropriate to the grade level being taught. The Big Dipper, Little Dipper, Leo, and Draco are the easiest constellations to recognize. Identify each with a neatly lettered label. For older students, also include a brief written description.

**ADAPTATIONS:** (1) Change the caption to "Let Me Tell You" and remove the constellations. On each of five large white laminated stars, write a word or phrase, such as "TV program," "food," "story," "game," or "super hero," using a temporary transparency marker. Each day select one of these as the subject for a speaking or writing activity. Topics suggested by students will make this display usable for many weeks. (2) Change the sky to light blue and the border to dark blue. Replace the constellations with cloud formations that are attached to the board with straight pins and pulled away from board to the pin heads. Label each cloud (i.e., stratus, cumulus, cirrus). (3) Use the blue background and border again. Change the caption to "Sky-High Stories." Display students' creative writing done on small white paper clouds by arranging them on the board in an attractive nonsymmetrical pattern.

**SUBJECT AREA:** Science.

**PURPOSE:** To provide an opportunity to monitor and record weather data.

**MONEY SAVER:** Secondhand sunglasses, a straw hat, sandals, and a swimsuit add a summery touch to this display. Obtain grocery sacks from supermarkets for constructing the tree.

**ADDING DIMENSIONALITY:** The seasonal attire worn by the monkey is real. To make the tree, cut open large grocery sacks, crinkle them repeatedly, and then twist them into long snake-like shapes. These can be used to construct the trunk and limbs.

**COLOR SCHEME:** Border = bright yellow; background = light green; monkey and barrel = brown; worm = red; chart = beige; leaves = dark green; lettering = bright yellow.

**CONSTRUCTION HINTS:** Cut the monkey from fun fur or bathroom carpeting with a long pile. Make the nose from felt or dull-finished plastic or leather, stuffing

it so that it protrudes. Cover a ball with lengths of rug yarn and make one large braid to form the worm's body. Prepare a set of cards containing words that are commonly used to describe weather conditions (e.g., windy, sunny, humid, freezing, etc.). Make a laminated chart on which to record weather data for a one-week period.

**CONTENT HINTS:** Each day, the class decides what the weather is like and the appropriate card is attached to the board. Daily readings of temperature, barometric pressure, and wind velocity and direction are made and recorded on the chart with a temporary transparency marker. Weather information can be obtained from actual measuring instruments or, as an alternative, from TV or local newspapers.

**ADAPTATIONS:** This display may be used throughout the year. In the fall, place a thin jacket and matching hat on the monkey; a ski cap, flowing wool scarf, and mittens may be used for winter; and in spring a yellow slicker and rain hat are most appropriate. Omit leaves in winter; make them yellow, orange, and red in fall. If desired, base math or language arts activities on the charted information.

**EXPLORE THE WORLD OF COUSTEAU**

**SUBJECT AREA:** Science.

**PURPOSE:** To spark an interest in learning about marine biology.

**MONEY SAVER:** Locate a pair of child's swim fins and a pair of goggles for the dog to wear. Collect real seashells to scatter on the ocean floor.

**ADDING DIMENSIONALITY:** Attach two long, sturdy tabs to the bubbles so they will stick out from board. Fashion an oyster shell from heavy paper and position it so it buckles out from the board's surface.

**COLOR SCHEME:** Border = red; background = light blue water, light brown sand; bubbles = white; shark = gray; other objects = beige, mustard; lettering = red.

**CONSTRUCTION HINTS:** The "pearl" can be a glass or a clear plastic ball. Laminate the bubbles so they appear to be transparent. Make the shark using paper or fabric or locate an inflatable toy shark.

**CONTENT HINTS:** Strive to make the display appear tranquil and serene by avoiding the use of bright colors. Viewers should have a sensation of being under water.

**ADAPTATIONS:** (1) Use this as an end-of-the-year display and change the caption to "Summer Fun" or "Have a Safe Summer." (2) Change the caption to "Sea-faring Stories." Encourage creative writing by placing story starters that carry out the deep-sea theme on the bubbles. (3) Change the caption to "Swim, Swam, Swum" and use as a motivator for a unit on irregular verbs.

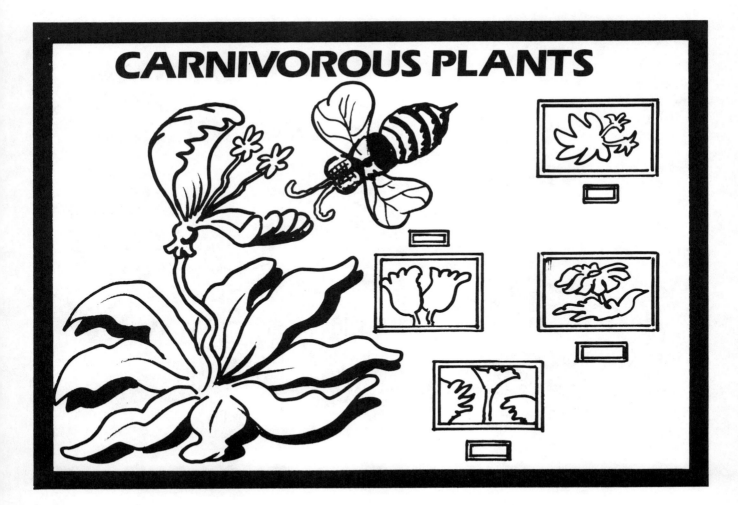

# CARNIVOROUS PLANTS

**SUBJECT AREA:** Science.

**PURPOSE:** To arouse interest in plant life.

**MONEY SAVER:** Locate photographs of carnivorous plants in magazines.

**ADDING DIMENSIONALITY:** Construct the bee from fuzzy fabric and stuff it as though you were making a small pillow. Pipe cleaners can serve as legs, and wings can be made by gluing cellophane to a wire form.

**COLOR SCHEME:** Border = green; background = yellow; bee = black, brown, yellow; plant = green with white flowers; lettering = orange.

**CONSTRUCTION HINTS:** Mount pictures of plants on orange posterboard, allowing for a ¼″–½″ border around each picture. The large plant may be made from paper or cardboard but is more attractive if fabric is glued to a cardboard form. For best results, dilute white glue with water and apply *thinly* to cardboard with a paint brush.

**CONTENT HINTS:** On white paper identify the plant in each of the four pictures. Include a brief description of each plant, if desired. Mount each of these on the same type of paper or board that the pictures are mounted on, leaving the same size orange border around the caption/description you used for the pictures. Place the captions above or below their corresponding pictures.

**ADAPTATIONS:** (1) Change the caption to "Pollination" and replace the pictures with illustrations of the steps in the pollination cycle, placing green arrows between steps to indicate progression. (2) Change the caption to "Plants of the Jungle." Mounted pictures should not be just of carnivorous plants. (3) Change the caption to "'Bee' Informed" and replace pictures with mounted newspaper and magazine articles of current interest. Change the display items frequently.

# ACTIVITIES FOR ALL SEASONS

WINTER　　SPRING　　SUMMER　　FALL

**SUBJECT AREA:** Science.

**PURPOSE:** To differentiate between the seasons of the year.

**MONEY SAVER:** Everything on this board can be constructed inexpensively using colored paper, wallpaper samples, and/or fabric remnants.

**ADDING DIMENSIONALITY:** Attach snowflakes, clouds, sun, and leaves to the board with straight pins and pull them away from the board to the heads of the pins.

**COLOR SCHEME:** Border = light blue; background = yellow; sun = yellow and orange; clouds = white and dark blue; snowflakes = white; leaves = yellow, red, orange; lettering = light blue.

**CONSTRUCTION HINTS:** As illustrated, there are many small objects on this board. Cut one blue and one white cloud and attach them to the board using the shadowing effect. If real leaves are used, they will need to be dried and preserved.

**CONTENT HINTS:** Select symbols for the display that represent each of the four seasons of the year; use the illustration above as a guide. If desired, collages made from magazine pictures may be substituted for skis, umbrella, sailboat, etc. Cut the collage in an interesting shape that conforms to the content of the pictures.

**ADAPTATIONS:** (1) Have children draw pictures of what they like to do during one of the seasons. Mount these on colorful paper and display them on the board. (2) Change the caption to "Holidays for All Seasons" and replace cutouts that illustrate activities with visuals dealing with holidays. (3) Similar adaptations can be made to depict the types of clothing worn during different seasons of the year or the birthdays of class members or of famous people. Change the caption accordingly.

**MAKE YOUR OWN COAT OF ARMS**

**SUBJECT AREA:** Social studies.

**PURPOSE:** To provide a vehicle for sharing cultural backgrounds.

**MONEY SAVER:** Search the family album for photographs to be displayed.

**ADDING DIMENSIONALITY:** Paper circles stuffed with green Easter basket grass and bits of nylon stockings make tacos look good enough to eat. Display an actual toy that is indicative of the culture represented.

**COLOR SCHEME:** Border = dark brown; background = light brown; triangle outline = dark brown; lettering = white and green.

**CONSTRUCTION HINTS:** The colors used inside the triangle should be symbolic of the culture being portrayed (e.g., Mexico—red, green, and white). Avoid using only pictures on the board; locate or construct three-dimensional objects for display. Cut two sets of letters. When mounting, offset the green letters by placing them on top of white letters to produce a shadow effect.

**CONTENT HINTS:** Here's an opportunity for students to share information about their heritage. They can construct displays similar to this one or can make individual coats of arms on poster board. Visualization of foods, crafts, sports, family, holidays, toys, and national symbols should be encouraged.

**ADAPTATIONS:** (1) Change the caption to "Windows on the World" and inside the triangle display pictures of people of a number of countries on a background of green, yellow, and orange. (2) Change the caption to "U.S.A. All the Way," and in the triangle use a red, white, and blue color scheme to display mounted pictures or collages of the six regions of this country. (3) Change the caption to "The Animal Kingdom" and using a green, yellow, and orange color scheme, display mounted pictures of reptiles, mammals, birds, etc. For each of these adaptations, select one of the colors in the triangle to repeat in the caption.

# LET'S TRAVEL

**SUBJECT AREA:**   Social studies.

**PURPOSE:**   To stimulate student interest in geographic locations.

**MONEY SAVER:**   Obtain brochures or booklets from travel agents, chambers of commerce, or the American Automobile Association. Write or use toll-free phone numbers to request materials from state tourist bureaus. Write to embassies for pamphlets. Use old road maps for lettering.

**ADDING DIMENSIONALITY:**   Make a pocket in the car trunk and fill it with travel information. Construct the driver using old nylon stockings. Place a visor cap on the figure. Cut plastic wagon wheels in half for the car tires.

**COLOR SCHEME:**   Border = green; background = light blue; car = dark blue; road = brown; grass = green; lettering = red, white, blue.

**CONSTRUCTION HINTS:**   Trace letters on old road maps, laminate both sides, cut out letters.

**CONTENT HINTS:**   Travel to a specific state, to different regions of the U.S., or to a specific country. Make caption more specific by changing it to "Let's Travel to . . ." Make assignments that encourage students to read travel brochures. Change reading materials frequently.

**ADAPTATIONS:**   This board can be used in most subject areas by having the caption read "Let's Travel to the . . ." (Zoo, Power Plant, Hospital). Include filmstrips, film loops, and slides, as well as written material in the trunk.

# HURRAY FOR DIFFERENCES

**SUBJECT AREA:**   Social studies.

**PURPOSE:**   To create an awareness of the differences among people of varying cultures.

**MONEY SAVER:**   Generally speaking, it will be necessary to purchase special materials to produce the rainbow and clouds.

**ADDING DIMENSIONALITY:**   The clouds are made from cotton batting or quilting material. The rainbow is most attractive if sewn from a satin-like material and stuffed like a pillow. Since this is quite time consuming and takes some sewing talent, crepe paper or colored paper may be used instead. To achieve the best results, it may be worthwhile to purchase a plastic or paper rainbow at a gift or novelty shop.

**COLOR SCHEME:**   Border = dark blue; background = light blue; pot = red; rainbow = yellow, orange, red, green, blue, violet; lettering = dark blue.

**CONSTRUCTION HINTS:**   The collage beneath the rainbow is constructed from magazine pictures and photographs. Make a pocket of felt.

**CONTENT HINTS:**   As a class or small-group project, have children locate magazine pictures and bring photographs from home to use in constructing a large collage containing faces of males and females of all ages and of many cultures. Incorporate this collage into the display as illustrated above. Discuss how people of different colors make a beautiful world, as does the rainbow.

**ADAPTATIONS:**   (1) Change the caption to "A Rainbow of Colors" and use the display as an introduction to a science unit on rain and rainbows. Replace the collage with felt raindrops, each of which is one of the colors of the rainbow. On top of these, attach slightly smaller white paper raindrops on which information about rain and rainbows is neatly written. (2) Change the caption to "Colorful Words" and place descriptive adjectives on the raindrops. (3) Change the caption to "A Rainbow of Inventors" and in place of raindrops display mounted pictures and verbal information about people who have developed objects or procedures to improve the quality of life. Border the information in rainbow colors.

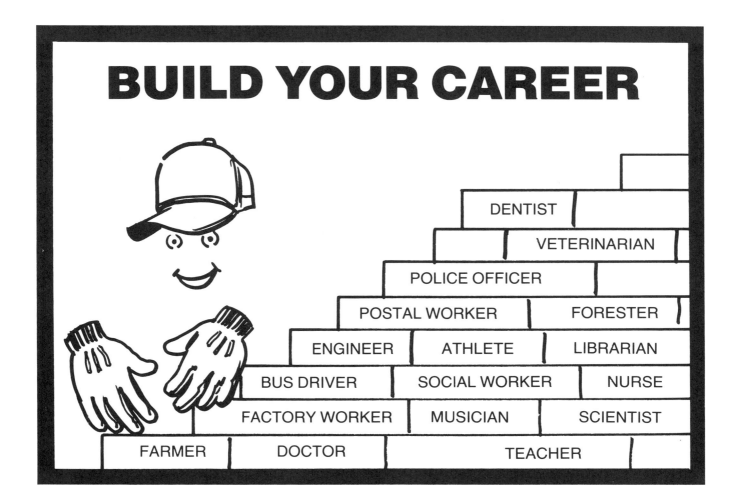

# BUILD YOUR CAREER

| | DENTIST | |
| | | VETERINARIAN |
| | POLICE OFFICER | |
| | POSTAL WORKER | FORESTER |
| ENGINEER | ATHLETE | LIBRARIAN |
| BUS DRIVER | SOCIAL WORKER | NURSE |
| FACTORY WORKER | MUSICIAN | SCIENTIST |
| FARMER | DOCTOR | TEACHER |

**SUBJECT AREA:**   Social studies.

**PURPOSE:**   To foster career awareness.

**MONEY SAVER:**   Use egg carton cups for the facial features. Pay half price at after-Christmas sales for brick-patterned crepe paper, or buy a roll of brick-patterned wallpaper.

**ADDING DIMENSIONALITY:**   The figure in this display is nondescript and is made of a cap, painted egg-carton cups, and a pair of gloves. The wall will appear to stick out from board if it is made from a corrugated carton that is covered with a brick pattern.

**COLOR SCHEME:**   Border = brown; background = brown; gloves = green; wall = red and white; lettering = yellow.

**CONSTRUCTION HINTS:**   Have students letter occupational titles on white "bricks."

**CONTENT HINTS:**   Use nonsexist occupational titles (e.g., police officer, not policeman). Use blue-collar and white-collar titles. These may be changed periodically to present a wide spectrum of occupations. Have students select an occupation, research it, present findings to the class, and post the title on the wall.

**ADAPTATIONS:**   (1) Change caption to "Build Good Health" and include words or pictures on the bricks that relate to physical fitness (exercise, sleep, roughage, etc.). (2) Change the caption to "Build Division Skills" and place math problems to be solved on the bricks ($12 \div 4 =$ , $8 \div 2 =$ ). (3) Change the caption to "Build Spelling Skills" and write the week's spelling words on the bricks. These are just a few of the many variations that are possible.

# DRUMS AROUND THE WORLD

**SUBJECT AREA:** Social studies.

**PURPOSE:** To increase awareness of the types and uses of drums in various cultures.

**MONEY SAVER:** The drum base is made from half of an empty institutional-size tin can or a round two-gallon ice cream container. Check the school cafeteria for both of these items. Select remnants of plastic upholstery fabric or pieces of a flannel-backed plastic tablecloth for the top and bottom of the drum. Borrow a set of drumsticks from the music teacher.

**ADDING DIMENSIONALITY:** Only the caption is not three-dimensional.

**COLOR SCHEME:** Border = orange; background = brown; drum = bright blue base with white top and bottom; notes = bright blue; musical staff = white; pocket = orange; lettering = orange.

**CONSTRUCTION HINTS:** Cover the drum base with paper. Cut a circle of plastic fabric that is about 2″ larger in diameter than the top of the drum base. Cut this circle in half. Approximately 1″ in from the circumference edge of each half, punch 4 or 5 holes, as illustrated. Attach the two halves to the drum and lace them together, as shown, with lanyard material, twine, or yarn. Heavy yarn can be used to form the musical staff. The notes can be made from the same material that covers the drum.

**CONTENT HINTS:** In the pocket place instructional cards that illustrate and describe the various types of drums used by Native Americans, Africans, Latin Americans, etc.

**ADAPTATIONS:** This display also may be used in music classes to emphasize differences and similarities in the use of musical instruments in a number of cultures. (1) Change the caption to "Sing Along." In the pocket place sheet music or pages of song lyrics and sing. (2) Change the caption to "Music, Music, Music," place activity cards that call for listening and reading in the pocket, and use in a learning center. (3) Change the color scheme to red, white, and blue and the caption to "The Spirit of '76."

**SUBJECT AREA:**   Social studies.

**PURPOSE:**   To aid in celebrating a fall holiday.

**MONEY SAVER:**   Remnants of wallpaper, ribbon, and fabric will help make this board noticeable.

**ADDING DIMENSIONALITY:**   Make the cat from fuzzy fabric and place a real bow around its neck. Allow the leaves on the pumpkin vines to stick out from the board by not pinning down their tips. The vines are curled paper strips.

**COLOR SCHEME:**   Border = black; background = dark green; pumpkins = orange; leaves and vines = light green; fence = beige; lettering = patchwork in orange, brown, green.

**CONSTRUCTION HINTS:**   Cut letters from patterned wallpaper or from cloth mounted on lightweight poster board. If desired, cut letters with pinking shears.

**CONTENT HINTS:**   Smiling faces on the pumpkins convey a message of humor and gaiety.

**ADAPTATIONS:**   (1) Use the caption "What's Cooking?" Replace the cat with a pocket containing laminated recipes for Halloween foods. Use these with math and/or language activities. (2) Change the caption to "Pumpkin Patch News" and replace the cat with a student-produced newspaper containing items about classroom or school happenings—an excellent way to practice a variety of language arts skills. Mount newspaper on orange poster-board, allowing for a ½″ border. (3) Change the caption to "Halloween Safety" and in place of the cat, post an attractive poster containing pointers for having a safe holiday. Border the poster in black.

**SUBJECT AREA:**   Social studies.

**PURPOSE:**   To promote research about the first Americans.

**MONEY SAVER:**   Purchase fabric remnants or use an old suede coat for the clothing. Collect tree branches for the top of the tepee.

**ADDING DIMENSIONALITY:**   Place a real feather in the headband; braid black yarn for hair; and if you can find them, place a pair of moccasins on the Native American's feet. Roll brown paper for logs.

**COLOR SCHEME:**   Border = brown; background = yellow; tepee and clothing = browns; rug = multicolored; lettering = orange.

**CONSTRUCTION HINTS:**   The clothing, the tepee, and the rug can all be made from paper if fabrics are not available. Suede or velour gives the appearance of animal skins.

**CONTENT HINTS:**   If desired, place authentic Native American symbols on the smoke clouds. Have students research and write compositions about Native Americans. These should reflect the fact that tribes live in different types of abodes, that the crafts differ from tribe to tribe, that among different tribes there are also commonalities. Students may wish to decorate their compositions with Native American symbols. Mount student papers around the edge of the display board for others to read.

**ADAPTATIONS:**   (1) Change the caption to "Say It with Pictures" and have children make Native American rugs by drawing authentic Native American symbols on brown paper grocery sacks that are crumpled repeatedly and then ironed. Protect the iron surface by covering the "rug" with brown paper. Do the ironing yourself or supervise students closely if they are using the iron. (2) Use this display to help introduce a unit on Plains Indians or the first Americans. Change the caption accordingly.

**FLIP FOR A CLEAN AMERICA**

**SUBJECT AREA:**  Affective education.

**PURPOSE:**  To encourage children to help keep the environment clean by not littering.

**MONEY SAVER:**  Save or collect all types of empty containers. Dress the figure in real clothing that has been donated, borrowed, or bought second hand. Ask the school custodian for a plastic trash bag.

**ADDING DIMENSIONALITY:**  Stuff the trash bag and trash can with newspaper. Top with boxes, food containers, and cans so that the large receptacles appear to be overflowing. Make the face from a nylon stocking stufed with cotton. Use tufts of yarn for the hair. Drape or stuff the clothing.

**COLOR SCHEME:**  Border = red; background = yellow; clothing = blue; lettering = red.

**CONSTRUCTION HINTS:**  Cut a real plastic trash can in half and help anchor it by suspending it from the ceiling with clear fishing line.

**CONTENT HINTS:**  Trash should include wrappers or containers of foods or objects of a variety of cultures. Children will take notice if fast-food and toy wrappers are included as part of the trash.

**ADAPTATIONS:**  (1) Change the caption to "Flip for Good Health" and in place of trash containers, mount two baskets or lightweight wooden crates (one cut in half). Fill these with plastic vegetables and fruits and containers from nutritious foods. (2) Change the caption to "Fraction Flip" and replace the trash bag and can with pies, squares, or rectangles that are divided into equal parts. Label with the appropriate fraction. (3) Remove the trash bag and can, move the child to the left of the board, and change the caption to "Shaping Up." Construct a wagon from colored paper circles, triangles, squares, and rectangles. Place a wagon handle in the child's hand.

**SUBJECT AREA:**  Affective education.

**PURPOSE:**  To remind students of appropriate classroom behavior.

**MONEY SAVER:**  Locate a secondhand kerchief; any color will do.

**ADDING DIMENSIONALITY:**  Drape the kerchief around the elephant's neck. Attach the caption to the board with straight pins, then pull the letters to the heads of the pins. Fringe green paper to form grass. If desired, place a hat on the elephant's head.

**COLOR SCHEME:**  Border = dark blue; background = light blue; elephant = gray; lettering = dark blue.

**CONSTRUCTION HINTS:**  This board is easy to construct because everything except the kerchief is made of paper. For the background, you may wish to select wallpaper or wrapping paper that has a small repeated pattern or narrow stripes.

**CONTENT HINTS:**  Below the caption, place an attractive poster listing classroom rules. These may be teacher determined or student generated.

**ADAPTATIONS:**  By changing the content of the poster, this display can be used as a reminder to students of rules, procedures, steps in a process, or the meaning of symbols or terms. Good for all subject areas.

**A STEADY PACE**

**FOR GOOD WORK**

**SUBJECT AREA:** Affective education.

**PURPOSE:** To encourage students to develop positive work habits.

**MONEY SAVER:** Collect squares of fabric that can be used to make the patchwork turtle shell.

**ADDING DIMENSIONALITY:** Fashion the turtle's cap from a circle of fabric with a drawstring sewn about 2″ from the perimeter. Construct the butterflies from brightly colored tissue paper; use plastic clothespins for bodies and pipe cleaners for antennae.

**COLOR SCHEME:** Border = white; background = yellow; turtle head and legs = dark green; shell = light-colored pastel prints; lettering = dark green.

**CONSTRUCTION HINTS:** Children may sew together squares for the turtle shell. They may also help make butterflies. Position cotton batting or a similar type of stuffing material under the fabric shell. Place these two layers over a slightly smaller cardboard shell. Staple excess fabric to the back of the cardboard form. Curled paper eyelashes add personality to the turtle.

**CONTENT HINTS:** This is a good springtime board. If desired, place the name of a "good" worker/helper for the day on each butterfly. Or, in place of butterflies, display the day's "good" student work.

**ADAPTATIONS:** (1) Use this display to guide children's TV viewing by changing the title to "Tilda Turtle's TV Tidbits" and posting the names of upcoming programs of value. (2) Change the caption to "Turtle Tidbits," omit the butterflies, and display interesting facts about turtles. (3) Again omit the butterflies and change the caption to "Turtle Tales." Have children write stories or poems about turtles. Display these. Remember to add a narrow border of a coordinating color around each story or item posted on the board.

# CLEAN UP AFTER YOURSELF

**SUBJECT AREA:** Affective education.

**PURPOSE:** To encourage students to take responsibility for maintaining work areas.

**MONEY SAVER:** Gather together old rulers, pencil stubs, inkless pens, and art supplies you have been collecting and meaning to throw out for years.

**ADDING DIMENSIONALITY:** The debris shown beneath the pig consists of a variety of papers, actual art, and writing supplies. Use half of a plastic pail for the paint pot. Empty 8-oz. tomato sauce cans with labels removed make good smaller paint containers. Curl paper for pig's tail.

**COLOR SCHEME:** Border = black; background = red; pig = light pink with black nose; lettering = black.

**CONSTRUCTION HINTS:** This is an easy board to construct because there is so little detail. Crumple newspaper and include it with the rest of the debris. Wash hands immediately after handling newspaper, or the printer's ink will end up everywhere! You may wish to use a red and white check or gingham pattern for the background.

**CONTENT HINTS:** Debris can include paint, paint brushes, twisted tubes of glue or paint, rulers, chalk, pencils, and pens. Let your imagination be your guide.

**ADAPTATIONS:** (1) For debris, substitute a big puddle for the pig to prance through, change the caption to "Pink Pigs Prefer Puddles," and use as an introduction to a discussion of colorful speech, alliteration, or tongue twisters. (2) Substitute food wrappers and containers for art supplies, change the caption to "Pig-Out Panic," and use as a motivator for a discussion on nutrition and snack foods. (3) Change the caption to "Don't Make a Pig of Yourself" and use it as part of a unit on figures of speech.

**SUBJECT AREA:** Affective education.

**PURPOSE:** To promote the development of positive behaviors.

**MONEY SAVER:** Locate a colorful umbrella. It is usable if some of the metal ribs are bent or broken.

**ADDING DIMENSIONALITY:** Cut the umbrella in half and anchor it to the board. The raindrops are attached to the board with straight pins and are pulled away from the board to the heads of the pins. Whiskers are made from pipe cleaners.

**COLOR SCHEME:** Border = white; background = slate blue; umbrella = bright colors; animals = pastel colors; lettering = black.

**CONSTRUCTION HINTS:** Letters on the umbrella must contrast sufficiently to be read with ease. Raindrops and puddles are made from aluminum foil mounted on lightweight cardboard. Either paper or fun fur may be used to form animals. If an umbrella cannot be located, construct one from pieces of art foam.

**CONTENT HINTS:** The expressions illustrated can be used to explore some of the reasons why smiles are contagious. After this, change the expression on the serious face to a smile.

**ADAPTATIONS:** Transform this display into a number of seasonal or weather boards. (1) Change the caption to "Snow" or "Winter," omit the umbrella, substitute snowflakes for raindrops, and place wool scarfs and ski caps on the animals. (2) Change the caption to "Welcome, Sunshine," remove puddles and raindrops, put sunglasses and bathing suits on the animals, and place sun rays in the upper right corner of the board. (3) Change the caption to "Fabulous Fall," place a pile of leaves under the animals' feet, and dress them in sweaters.

**SUBJECT AREA:** Affective education.

**PURPOSE:** To provide a showcase for student work and to encourage students to put forth their best efforts.

**MONEY SAVER:** This is an inexpensive board to prepare because it is made almost entirely of paper.

**ADDING DIMENSIONALITY:** Pieces of yarn or strips of paper are used to form the lion's mane and the end of its tail. Construct a large pencil (about ¾" in diameter) for the lion to hold by rolling a piece of paper into a tube. The eraser is a shorter tube of rolled paper of a contrasting color. Fashion the pencil tip by making a paper cone.

**COLOR SCHEME:** Border = orange; background = yellow; lion = brown; mane and tail = dark brown; pencil = light blue with a yellow tip and pink eraser; lettering = orange.

**CONSTRUCTION HINTS:** Surround each student paper being displayed with a ¼"–½" border of orange paper. Using wallpaper with a small repeated pattern for the letters or background is a welcome change from routinely used solid colors.

**CONTENT HINTS:** Change student papers selected for display daily. Attempt to post each child's work—not just excellent efforts, but those that show improvement, too.

**ADAPTATIONS:** (1) Change the caption to "Letter Perfect" and in place of student work, post examples of good manuscript or cursive writing for children to emulate. (2) Using this caption again, post examples of types of correspondence (i.e., friendly letter, thank you, letter of request) and label each with cutout letters that are smaller than those in the main caption. (3) Change the caption to "Something to Roar About" and replace student papers with news items describing positive achievements and happenings.

**GIVE A FLOWERFUL COMPLIMENT**

**SUBJECT AREA:** Affective education.

**PURPOSE:** To aid in the development of appropriate interpersonal behaviors.

**MONEY SAVER:** Fabric remnants and scraps may be used to produce colorful flowers and interesting animals.

**ADDING DIMENSIONALITY:** Whiskers are made from pipe cleaners, tails from yarn pompoms.

**COLOR SCHEME:** Border = brown; background = yellow; animals = brown and white; grass and leaves = green; flowers = red; lettering = red.

**CONSTRUCTION HINTS:** The entire board may be made from papers, but animals made from fuzzy fabric and tissue paper flowers are more alluring. Vinyl wallpaper in a wood grain pattern makes the tree look realistic.

**CONTENT HINTS:** Children may wish to make flowers for display. Select a pattern and directions that are appropriate for the maturity of your students.

**ADAPTATIONS:** (1) To provide motivation for another positive behavior, change the caption to "Sharing Is Caring." (2) This becomes an environmental-awareness display when the caption is changed to "The Woods Belongs to Them." (3) Replace the flower in the right corner with a basket full of laminated paper flowers on which activities or tasks are specified. Where appropriate, provide answers. Good in most subject areas. Change caption accordingly.

**SUBJECT AREA:** Affective education.

**PURPOSE:** To help foster positive interpersonal relationships.

**MONEY SAVER:** Locate secondhand T-shirts and scraps of dark-colored felt for the cap and facial features.

**ADDING DIMENSIONALITY:** Loosely stuff the shirts with tissue paper. Use a bathroom rug for fuzzy bodies and faces.

**COLOR SCHEME:** Border = brown; background = orange; shirts = pastel colors; bears = brown; lettering = yellow.

**CONSTRUCTION HINTS:** "Monogram" the shirts with bookbinding tape, iron-on transfers, or cutouts. The sun is made from paper.

**CONTENT HINTS:** Animals appear to be more realistic if they are brown, but are more whimsical if made with pastel colors. If pastels are used, select color of shirts and background accordingly.

**ADAPTATIONS:** (1) Place straw hats and sunglasses on the animals and change the caption to "Summer Safety." Use the display to introduce the hazards of exposing the skin to excessive amounts of sun. (2) Change the caption to "Summer Fun" or "Have a Super Summer," place sand pails in the animals' paws, and display just before school is out for the year.

**PLEASE DON'T BREAK THE RULES**

RULES

**SUBJECT AREA:**   Affective education.

**PURPOSE:**   To remind students of appropriate classroom behavior.

**MONEY SAVER:**   The T-shirt, shorts, socks, shoes, child's basketball hoop, and ball should be obtained secondhand. A foam rubber ball works well.

**ADDING DIMENSIONALITY:**   Dress the girl in real clothing that contrasts with the background color of the display. Use black or brown yarn for hair.

**COLOR SCHEME:**   Border = dark blue; background = light blue; lettering = dark blue.

**CONSTRUCTION HINTS:**   To prevent damaging the board itself, attach the basket over the edge of the board or use clear fishing line to hang the hoop from the ceiling.

**CONTENT HINTS:**   Place copies of classroom rules in the pocket so students may help themselves. Or replace the pocket with a poster listing classroom rules. The basketball may rest in the basket or may appear to be heading toward the basket.

**ADAPTATIONS:**   (1) Remove the handout pocket, change the caption to "Raise the Score," and let children help make a border from small paper basketballs bearing children's names. Award these for each book read or for each improved assignment completed. (2) Change the caption to "Today's Pro," use as a reward for a job well done, and replace the pocket with one big paper basketball on which a student's name is placed daily. (3) Change the caption to "Division Is a Ball" and place division problems on 8 to 10 paper basketballs that are arranged attractively in front of the girl. Make this activity self-checking.

**KEEP THE SPARKLE IN YOUR SMILE**

**SUBJECT AREA:** Health.

**PURPOSE:** To promote good dental hygiene.

**MONEY SAVER:** String white styrofoam packing material with a needle and heavy thread to form a stream of toothpaste. The toothpaste on the brush is the same packing material that can usually be obtained for free at a local business or at the school district's central receiving office.

**ADDING DIMENSIONALITY:** The toothbrush is actually a snow brush used for cleaning windshields. Remove the scraper from the end of the brush stick, if yours has one. Fashion a three-dimensional toothpaste tube from paper. Loosely stuff it with tissue paper or newspaper.

**COLOR SCHEME:** Border = dark blue; background = light blue; tube of toothpaste = yellow with orange and white detail; beaver = brown with white belly; lettering = orange.

**CONSTRUCTION HINTS:** Fun fur makes the beaver appealing; as an alternative, use a bathroom scatter rug. Glue glitter on the word "SPARKLE."

**CONTENT HINTS:** If desired, the toothpaste tube may be designed after a popular brand. Change the colors of the tube as needed.

**ADAPTATIONS:** (1) Change the caption to "Smile Awhile" and make a stream of toothpaste out of adding machine paper on which are printed jokes for viewers to read and enjoy. (2) Change the caption to "Writing with Sparkle" and place descriptive or action words on a stream of toothpaste that is also made from adding machine paper. (3) Change the caption to "It All Stacks Up," use just the beaver, and on the right-hand side of the board display mounted pictures and reading material that explain how and why beavers build dams. Mounts should be bright green or yellow.

**SUBJECT AREA:**   Health.

**PURPOSE:**   To promote proper nutrition.

**MONEY SAVER:**   Save empty food containers for display. Purchase the bandanna secondhand.

**ADDING DIMENSIONALITY:**   Display real food and empty food containers. Pipe cleaners can be used to form the tiger's whiskers.

**COLOR SCHEME:**   Border = black; background = light blue; tiger = orange and black stripes, white face and chest; bandanna = red; circles = black; letters = orange with black shadow.

**CONSTRUCTION HINTS:**   Cut a black and an orange set of letters. Shadow letters by offsetting orange letters on top of black so that black letters are showing to the right of the orange. Glue real foods and pin food containers to the paper circles. Eggshells, pasta, milk and yogurt cartons, nuts, and cereal boxes are suggested.

**CONTENT HINTS:**   On each circle represent one of the four food groups. Foods displayed should be those eaten by people from a variety of cultures.

**ADAPTATIONS:**   (1) Change the caption to "Our Class is Gr-r-reat" and mount photographs of class members and/or activities on circles (document class activities and projects with an instant camera. (2) Use this caption again and display student work on circles. (3) Change the caption to "Verbs Are Gr-r-reat" and around the circles display mounted drawings or pictures that illustrate action verbs. Be sure to label each visual with the appropriate word.

**SUBJECT AREA:** Health.

**PURPOSE:** To promote healthful living.

**MONEY SAVER:** Obtain fabric remnants to clothe the detective and construct the animal.

**ADDING DIMENSIONALITY:** Use a real magnifying glass. Dress the detective in a real hat and gloves. Make the lion's hair, mane, and the tip of its tail from yarn or fun fur. Stuff the belly of the animal. Jiggly eyes are attention getters.

**COLOR SCHEME:** Border = dark green; background = light blue; jacket = yellow; pants, hat = brown; animal = beige, white, brown; footprints = white; lettering = pink.

**CONSTRUCTION HINTS:** The animal's body may be made from paper, but it will be much more attractive if it is made from fun fur. Clothing may be made of either paper or fabric.

**CONTENT HINTS:** Place the name of a healthful food or positive health habit on each footprint.

**ADAPTATIONS:** (1) Change the caption to "Tracking Math Facts," place a problem on one print and its answer on another, and attach each pair to the board so that only the problems show. Students can lift the top print to reveal the answers. (2) Change the caption to "Tracking Down Compound Words" and place compound words on footprints. (3) Change the caption to "It's a Mystery" and on the footprints place parts of a story in a scrambled order. Have students rearrange the footprints so that the story makes sense— this is a good sequencing and comprehension activity. Change the story as needed.

# SPORTS FOR ALL SORTS

**SUBJECT AREA:** Health.

**PURPOSE:** To encourage participation in physical activity.

**MONEY SAVER:** Secure a secondhand rattle, plastic bat, and tennis balls. Dress the child with the bat in real T-shirt, shorts, tennis shoes, and socks. Place a whistle on a string around his neck.

**ADDING DIMENSIONALITY:** Cut the plastic bat and tennis balls in half and attach to the board with T-pins. Fringe green paper for grass. Curl strips of yellow paper for the baby's hair. There's a real golf ball in the grass.

**COLOR SCHEME:** Border = light blue; background = yellow; clothing = blue and white; shoes = red; pennant = red; lettering = light blue.

**CONSTRUCTION HINTS:** The brown football and white volleyball are made from paper. Most of the display may be constructed from paper but will be more enticing if real objects and clothing are used. Don't forget to include the pieces of black paper that show the movement of the balls.

**CONTENT HINTS:** Notice that the children represent different ethnic groups. The child with the bat could be a girl or a boy.

**ADAPTATIONS:** (1) Change the caption to "Teamwork Works" and use to encourage cooperation. (2) Change the caption to "Suit Out" to remind students of proper attire for physical activity. (3) Use the caption "It Happens Every Spring" and omit balls and equipment that do not deal with baseball. Place baseball caps on the children's heads.

**JUMP INTO FITNESS**

**SUBJECT AREA:** Health.

**PURPOSE:** To emphasize the value of physical activity for good health.

**MONEY SAVER:** Borrow a child's basketball, hoop, and jump rope.

**ADDING DIMENSIONALITY:** Hair is made from yarn. Dress figures in real sports attire or uniforms.

**COLOR SCHEME:** Border = bright blue; background = yellow; clothing = red and white; lettering = bright blue.

**CONSTRUCTION HINTS:** The children's faces and extremities are made from paper. To avoid placing hooks in your display board, attach the basketball hoop over the edge of the board or support it from the ceiling with transparent fishing line.

**CONTENT HINTS:** The boy is black—use brown paper for his skin. Use peach or beige for the girl's skin; avoid using white. Uniforms in local team colors will capture viewers' attention.

**ADAPTATIONS:** (1) Change the caption to "Go for It." Remove the child jumping rope and the small basketball hoop; construct a large basketball hoop that sticks out from the board. Attach a net to this—part of an old volleyball net works well. Every time a child completes a book or reading assignment, place his or her name on a small paper basketball and mount it in or near the basket. (2) Change the caption to "Jump Rope Jingles" and remove the girl, the basket, and the ball. In their place, post mounted "poems to jump rope by" and use as a vehicle for teaching poetry or rhyming words. (3) Place the caption "Jump into Verbs" at the top of the board and replace one of the figures with a laminated piece of white poster board on which the teacher or students write verbs with a temporary transparency marker. The same idea can be adapted for the other seven parts of speech.

**SUBJECT AREA:** Art.

**PURPOSE:** To arouse interest in participating in art activities.

**MONEY SAVER:** Borrow real paint brushes from an artist or art teacher. The dog is wearing a real beret.

**ADDING DIMENSIONALITY:** Place brushes in the pocket of the smock. The smock is made of cloth.

**COLOR SCHEME:** Border = bright blue; background = yellow; smock = blue or red; bird = yellow; dog = white; lettering = bright blue.

**CONSTRUCTION HINTS:** If necessary, the entire board may be constructed of paper. Do include real brushes, however. Dip the brush to be placed in the dog's paw in tempera paint and allow to dry.

**CONTENT HINTS:** Both the bird and the dog are standing in puddles of paint. Place a variety of irregular swatches of color on the pallet in the dog's left paw. The spots on the smock are paint spills.

**ADAPTATIONS:** (1) Use this board in an art center. Raise the caption and attach an envelope in which are placed laminated project or task cards. (2) Change the caption to "Create!" Make paint brushes out of paper and place story starters on each brush. Good for a writing center. (3) Change the caption to "Get into the Arts," raise it, and post a calendar of upcoming community or school arts activities and performances (drama, dance, music, etc.). Mount on red poster board or paper, leaving ¼″ border all the way around the calendar.

## CREATE YOUR OWN PARADISE

**SUBJECT AREA:** Art.

**PURPOSE:** To provide a vehicle for creative expression.

**MONEY SAVER:** Make the curtain rod from an old broom handle. Rods and curtains may be purchased for little cost at garage sales.

**ADDING DIMENSIONALITY:** Use brackets to suspend the curtain rod without putting holes in the board or suspend the broom handle from the ceiling with clear nylon fishing line. Place cafe-type curtains on the rod. Use draped fabric for boat sails.

**COLOR SCHEME:** Border = red; background = light blue; curtains = beige; boats = brown with white sails; sun = yellow; lettering = red.

**CONSTRUCTION HINTS:** Curtains may be made by placing 2″ hems in a lightweight fabric remnant or piece of a bedsheet. The paradise scene can be paper sculpture, a mural, a collage, etc.

**CONTENT HINTS:** The teacher can construct the first scene, and individual students or groups can prepare subsequent ones. "Paradise" can relate to a place to be, a way of life, an "ideal" school, or a favorite party. Have students write stories or poems to accompany their "paradise."

**ADAPTATIONS:** (1) Change the caption to "Sail into the New Year." Have students write New Year's resolutions on small paper boats. Fasten boats to the board with an accordian-fold "spring." (2) Use the same caption. At the beginning of the school year, have students construct little boats on which they place their names. Have an instant camera handy to take photos. Glue these onto the boats so that everyone can learn names. (3) Change the caption to "The World of Water" and add sea creatures to the scene.

**SUBJECT AREA:** Art.

**PURPOSE:** To spark interest in participating in art activities.

**MONEY SAVER:** Clothe the artist in a child's smock or a man's shirt that is borrowed or obtained second-hand. Ask an artist or art teacher to lend you some paint brushes.

**ADDING DIMENSIONALITY:** Place real brushes in the artist's hands and a real beret on his head. The dog's nose is an oval stuffed with filling and attached to the face.

**COLOR SCHEME:** Border = orange; background = yellow; clothing and canvas = orange; dog = white with a blue nose; easel = brown; word bubble = light blue; lettering = orange.

**CONSTRUCTION HINTS:** The easel is constructed from strips of paper. The "canvas" may be made from poster board or from a picture frame to which cloth has been stapled.

**CONTENT HINTS:** For young children, it may be more appropriate if the caption is changed to "Ah, Art."

**ADAPTATIONS:** (1) Change the caption to "Our Rules" and for the dog canvas substitute an attractive poster containing a list of expected student behaviors. (2) Change the caption to "Today!" and replace the "canvas" with a poster or flip chart listing daily assignments or schedules for activity centers, learning stations, or computer activities. Attach a wooden dowel to the board to hold the "canvas." (3) Change the caption to "This Week!" and in place of the "canvas," post special happenings for the week—discussing this on Monday morning is a good way to set the stage for things to come.

**FUN WITH COLORS**

**SUBJECT AREA:** Art.

**PURPOSE:** To aid in color recognition and identification.

**MONEY SAVER:** White garden gloves and basket should be obtained secondhand. The background can be made from large grocery sacks whose bottoms have been removed.

**ADDING DIMENSIONALITY:** Gather white fabric to form ruffles. Make the clown's hair from yarn pompoms. Use the same yarn for balloon strings. Large pompoms decorate the front of the clown's suit. The gloves are real.

**COLOR SCHEME:** Border = orange; background = light brown; clown suit = yellow with orange dots; hair and balloon strings = bright orange; hat = black; shoes = red; lettering = orange.

**CONSTRUCTION HINTS:** The clown on the bicycle is made from one piece of cardboard on which colored papers are glued and, where necessary, poster paints are applied. Select cardboard that is not too thick to cut with your scissors. Balloons are made of felt.

**CONTENT HINTS:** Each of the crayons in the basket contains the name of the color of one of the balloons (red, orange, yellow, green, blue, purple) and is made from white cardboard. Print the name of a color on each and laminate. Back each with a piece of regular-grain sandpaper so that it will adhere to the balloons. This display can be used by the teacher to reinforce the names of colors or by individual students or small groups to practice naming colors. Make this activity self-checking by placing a dot of the appropriate color on the back of each crayon.

**ADAPTATIONS:** (1) Change the caption to "Reading Is a Circus," have children write book reports on balloon-shaped paper, and replace felt balloons with these. (2) Change the caption to "A Circus of Stories" and display stories written by students on balloon shapes. (3) Change the caption to "Fun with Numbers" and place math facts on balloons.